DO YOU HAVE WHAT IT TAKES TO BE A SLASH?

Have you ever said any of the following?

A. "I dream of leaving my day job—or at least taking some time off—so that I can pursue other passions."

B. "I'm happiest when I'm juggling tasks. Sometimes I do my best thinking when I put a project aside to work on something else for a while."

C. "I need a career that engages me fully—but is flexible enough that I can spend time with my family or doing other things that nurture me."

D. "I often feel pulled in many directions—not because I can't focus, but because I have so many interests and ideas."

E. "I'm comfortable with new beginnings. In fact, if I do the same thing for too long, I become bored by the lack of challenges."

If you agree with one or more of the above statements, a slash career could be right for you. In fact, you're probably already on your way to one. In today's increasingly elastic workplace, people with curiosity, vision, and a streak of independence can reject a conventional job—and custom-blend all their skills and interests into the slash careers of their dreams.

"For those of us (all of us) who have way more than one goal/passion/talent in life, this is the ultimate guide! Right now you're holding the best advice of more than 100 folks who've done it already. Better get out your thank-you cards, because you'll be writing one to Marci Alboher before you finish chapter 3!"

—**Keith Ferrazzi,**
CEO/speaker/entrepreneur/author of *Never*
Eat Alone: And Other Secrets to Success, One
Relationship at a Time

"A must-read for anyone wanting to successfully navigate multiple callings."

—**Gregg Levoy, author of** *Callings: Finding and*
Following an Authentic Life

"Marci Alboher presents a descriptive and informative picture of a contemporary approach to building a career. . . . [This book] provides hope, inspiring case studies, and tangible tips for people who want to combine multiple interests and skills into a completely fulfilling career."

—**Julie Jansen, author of** *I Don't Know What I*
Want, But I Know It's Not This **and** *You Want Me*
to Work with Who?

"Written for those people who have multiple skills and interests, ONE PERSON/MULTIPLE CAREERS provides a winning strategy for both surviving and prospering in today's changing economy. A quick and interesting read with plenty of examples, the book will have a long-term impact on those who want to pursue several different careers simultaneously or in quick succession. It will help bring direction and sanity to multitaskers who are skillful at many things and want to figure out how to have it all."

—**Bill Coplin, author of** *10 Things Employers*
Want You to Learn in College: The Know-How
You Need to Succeed

"Your ability to identify and fully exploit all your talents is essential to maximizing your success. This book shows you, step-by-step, how to fulfill your true potential."

—Brian Tracy, author of *The Way to Wealth*

"Having multiple occupations is not only feasible but often fulfilling. There are some really interesting stories in here of personal triumph over the mundane and routine."

—Abby Wilner, researcher/speaker/webmaster/ coauthor of *Quarterlife Crisis*

"Insightful . . . essential for anyone trying to find time to pursue multiple passions."

—Laura Stack, speaker/mom/author of *Find More Time: How to Get Things Done at Home, Organize Your Life, and Feel Great About It*

"No one likes to be pigeonholed or put in a box. Marci helps us see that in our quest for fulfillment we can be many different things, all wrapped up in one authentic person!"

—Rebecca Zucker, founding partner of Next Step Partners

"I really like this book—especially the concrete examples of how 'The Slash Effect' can help you build your own business while maintaining security at the same time. Not only that, Alboher may have cracked the code for how to successfully integrate all our passions into multiple careers in a meaningful and profitable way."

—Michael Port, author of *Book Yourself Solid: The Fastest, Easiest, and Most Reliable System for Getting More Clients*

"Marci Alboher is the Walt Whitman of the new world of work. She realizes that we are large, that we contain multitudes. With deftly told stories and plenty of smart advice, Alboher shows how multiple professions and multiple identities can converge into a unified—and better—life. If what you do feels out of sync with who you are, this may be the most important book you read this year."

—**Daniel H. Pink, author of** *A Whole New Mind* **and** *Free Agent Nation*

/ / /

ONE PERSON
MULTIPLE CAREERS

A NEW MODEL FOR
WORK/LIFE SUCCESS

MARCI ALBOHER
AUTHOR/SPEAKER/COACH

WARNER
BUSINESS
BOOKS™

NEW YORK   BOSTON

Warner Business Books
Hachette Book Group USA
1271 Avenue of the Americas
New York, NY 10020

Visit our Web site at www.HachetteBookGroupUSA.com.

Warner Business Books is an imprint of Warner Books, Inc.

Printed in the United States of America

First Edition: February 2007

10 9 8 7 6 5 4 3 2 1

Warner Business Books is a trademark of Time Warner Inc. or an affiliated company. Used under license by Hachette Book Group USA, which is not affiliated with Time Warner Inc.

Library of Congress Cataloging-in-Publication Data

Alboher, Marci.
    One person/multiple careers : a new model for work/life success / Marci Alboher. — 1st ed.
        p.   cm.
    Includes index.
    ISBN-13: 978-0-446-69697-5
    ISBN-10: 0-446-69697-8
  1. Supplementary employment. 2. Job satisfaction. I. Title.
    HD5854.5.A43   2007
    650.1—dc22
                                                    2006019193

Book design and text composition by Anne Ricigliano

CONTENTS / / / / /

In memory of:

EMANUEL ALBOHER

(born December 28, 1930)

who taught me to embrace all aspects of life.

And for:

EMANUEL ALBOHER

(born December 28, 2005)

who will keep that spirit alive for all of us.

ACKNOWLEDGMENTS / / / / /

Writing this book was, above all, a great way to spend the last couple of years. It gave me the chance to be a fly on the wall of many an office, as well as the many other spots people are lucky enough to call their workplaces. I met with slashes in towering skyscrapers, restaurant kitchens, cafes and coffeehouses, living rooms, yoga and acupuncture studios, medical offices, television studios, health clubs, a publishing company situated on an apple orchard, and at the best table of the Grill Room at the Four Seasons restaurant in New York City.

It also gave me an excuse to travel and a ready-made conversation topic. I normally talk to strangers, but for a time, I did it with a singular focus, engaging everyone I met on a subject that pretty much anyone can relate to—work. Most important, it allowed me to get to know some extraordinary people and to completely enjoy myself while doing something that qualified as work.

It takes a village to write a book, or at least it did for me. These are my villagers. My parents, who made me feel like I could do anything, gave me the formal education neither of them had and served as role models of the limitless opportunities for reinventing oneself time and again. Chris Kenneally and Sarah Milstein turned me into a writer during our weekly "goils" meetings and edited me tough, even when it hurt. Jay, whose love arrived in the final months of this project, gave me a very good reason to shut down at the end of the work day. He also listened with convincing enthusiasm as I spun tales about the inspiring people who were keeping me awake at night. Carrie, my surrogate sister, kept me fit during our work-outs in Central Park and gave me daily exposure to the ins and outs of living a slash life. My idea team helped me tinker and tweak the slash concept till it made sense: Susan Brennan, Amy Sandler, Ryan Nerz, Ricky Opaterny, Heidi Levin, Jennifer Dinn Korman, Belinda Plutz, Michael Melcher, Ellen Maguire, Deborah Epstein Henry, Stephanie Gunning, and Cathy Boyle. Gary, who will always have a place in my life, supported me in my career reinventions and fed me more slashes and workplace articles than I could keep up with. Then there were my men-tors, editors, and literary lights: Susan Shapiro, Charles Salzberg, Brent Bowers, Marie Brennar, Mike Winkleman, and Audrey McGinn. Talia Cohen brought this book to life, courting and supporting me the way I'd always dreamed an agent would. Dan Ambrosio "got" the concept of slash from our first meeting and had the wisdom to know that this book needed to explain not only the whys but also the hows of building a slash life. The entire team at Warner Books, especially Kallie Shimek with her copyediting wizardry, showed me that there is a lot more to publishing and selling a book than writing its text. My assis-tants, Laura Covelli and Yona Silverman, my students, and my writing clients taught me so much by letting me teach them.

And finally, there were all the slashes who opened up their homes, their workspaces, and their lives to me; especially Angela Williams, who began as a journalist's dream source and evolved into a friend and spiritual presence in my life. They took time out of their complicated lives to talk to me about their goals, their passions, and their struggles. They stayed in touch: e-mailing about professional accomplishments, updating me about changes in their personal and working lives, and inviting me to watch them at work, to hear them perform or speak, and even (in Angela's case) to a wedding.

INTRODUCTION ⁄ ⁄ ⁄ ⁄ ⁄ ⁄

A single fixed identity is a liability today. It only makes people more vulnerable to sudden changes in economic conditions. The most successful and healthy among us now develop multiple identities, managed simultaneously, to be called upon as conditions change. Recent research also suggests that developing multiple identities is one of the best buffers we can erect against mental and physical illness.

—Gail Sheehy, *New Passages: Mapping Your Life Across Time*

Angela Williams inspired me to write this book. In 2000, I met Angela at a conference for women lawyers in Washington, D.C. A prominent attorney who had worked for the Senate subcommittee that oversaw President Clinton's impeachment trial, she arrived at the podium to give a talk about the state of women in the legal profession. When she introduced herself to the audience, she began with an apology: "Please disregard the material you have about me in the agenda." The lawyers in the room rifled through the binders. The biography on Ms. Williams was all about her life as a Baptist minister. "My assistant inserted the bio for my other life," she explained. "Today, I'm here as a lawyer." I decided to track her down during the cocktail hour to learn more about what she meant. When I did, she intrigued me further with her comments. "I'm the one who puts them in jail in the morning and prays for them at night," she began.

After meeting at that conference, Angela and I began a series of conversations about what it means for her to be a lawyer/minister and to lead a working life with a slash in the middle of it. She talked about why she decided to travel down two seemingly divergent paths, and how she handles everything from time management to adhering to two codes of professional ethics.

Though we often spoke about the ease with which she managed her dual roles, it wasn't until I experienced the Clark Kent transformation firsthand that I understood how seamlessly she did it.

Over the years, Angela and I became friends, and it was in that capacity that I confided in her about a personal struggle—my husband and I had separated after a twelve-year marriage. Instantly, she assumed the role of spiritual advisor, lending me an ear and comforting me with her booming, melodious voice. She checked in on me each week to see how I was doing and to inspire me with stories of people who overcame periods of hardship.

Months later, when I told her that my husband and I had reached an impasse and would be divorcing, she immediately switched gears and began peppering me with questions about my legal and financial well-being. Though I knew Angela first as a lawyer, I was momentarily surprised to hear her focus on business and money when we had been talking only about emotions and feelings.

Angela is so adept at toggling between her different orientations that she doesn't see it as unusual or disjointed. In fact, she considers her two vocations different ways of expressing the same core values that inform her life. She says she is merely being herself, in all the various things that she does and in all the various roles she plays.

In my first interview with Angela for a *New York Times* article, she put it this way: "The interaction between my two professions is so clear. In fact, if you look at the legal profession and the core of Christianity, the one common thread is justice. It dates back to Biblical times, when priests were the jurists who listened to disputes and rendered decisions." Later she added: "The problem is that most people compartmentalize their lives. I have found a way to successfully integrate who I am as an authentic person in everything that I do."

Before long, I started to notice slashes everywhere—from unexpected career couplers like Angela to celebrities like Sean Combs/P. Diddy (rapper/entrepreneur/actor/activist) to old-fashioned moonlighters who pick up another job to generate extra cash (like a cop/landscaper I know who calls his business Lawn Enforcement) and others starting full-fledged businesses while hanging on to their day jobs for the health insurance and camaraderie. I met *über*volunteers who spend so much time in a do-gooder or philanthropic activity that they treat it as a second career, artists whose day jobs become dream jobs, and parents who are as likely these days to be mom/doctors as mom/PTA presidents.

My interest in slashes soon blossomed into a full-blown obsession. With each week's reading of magazines and news-papers, I clipped articles that described people with slashes. Whenever I mentioned the concept to friends and colleagues, they offered me names of slashes in their circles, confirming my suspicion that I was onto something.

I found slashes all over the United States and beyond. In Cambridge, Massachusetts, I spent time with Robert Childs, a psychotherapist/violin maker. In Seattle, I encountered Karen Rispoli, a life coach/bus driver/private investigator. Back home in New York City, I met Ann Guttman, a top-tier real estate agent who is a professional French horn player; her husband, Steve, is in the band Blood, Sweat & Tears and is a practicing psychoanalyst. Dawn Davide, based in New Mexico, divides her time between her salon where she styles hair two days a week and her booming home construction business. I even noticed the slashes in my immediate circle, like my childhood best friend, Carrie Lane, who is a Pilates instructor/art consultant/author.

Against this backdrop, I developed my own slash identity. In late 1999 I gave up practicing law after nearly a decade in that field. Soon after, I sat down with career coach Belinda Plutz to help me figure out a life after the law. She asked me what I wanted to do and I listed about ten occupations. "You seem a little too restless to do just one thing. You'll probably have a composite career," she said confidently. I had never heard the term before, but I was immediately comforted by it. Settling back into a single-track career seemed stifling and uncreative.

In about four years, I put together the various elements that became my new working life. Having always wanted to write, I began taking classes to become a journalist. Before long, I started publishing articles, first for legal trade magazines and then for national publications like the *New York Times*. Writing articles led to the other slashes in my career—teaching, coaching other writers, and public speaking. The process seemed organic, yet it took me a while to figure out how to integrate the different parts of my working life into a coherent whole.

Pursuing multiple vocations is by no means new. From Leonardo da Vinci, artist/inventor, to Benjamin Franklin, whose work included publishing, politics, and the emerging technology of his day, slash careerists have always existed at the highest strata of achievement. Likewise, in nonprofessional sectors, people have commonly taken on numerous jobs. What's new is that huge swaths of the population are being swept up in "The Slash Effect"—creating personalized careers that can only be described with the use of slashes. Why is that?

I had so many other questions. At what point does a hobby grow up and become a second career? Why does it have cachet to have a slash in your working life? Can you prepare for a career that allows for exploration of divergent interests, or does it just naturally occur when people follow their passions? Why is it that so many slashes manage to achieve great success within their multiple fields? Most of all, why do slashes seem more satisfied with their careers—and less oppressed by them—than those who hold just one job?

As I talked to more people, I began to get a few answers. The time we have to build a career is suddenly more expansive than it's ever been; we're simply living and working longer. And we all know that joining up with a large company where we will labor until retirement is no longer a viable plan. We're delaying marriage and children, creating longer periods of laying down our career foundations before family obligations interfere. We're collecting all kinds of educational training and life experience. We're a nation of entrepreneurs. Then there's the technology factor—so much of the work that's done today can be done *anywhere*; when your job is portable, it's that much easier to take on another one.

For as long as most people can remember, building a career has been equated with the notion of settling down, the way you'd think about marriage after playing the field. It's been about answering the "What do you want to be when you grow up?" question adoringly asked when we are small, but dogging us for a committed answer as we become adults. What the question doesn't allow for is that most of us cannot answer it with a singular response.

In formal interviews and informal discussions, at professional conferences and adult education classes, and at work/life balance meetings and at dinner parties, I've now tracked hundreds of people whose working lives fall somewhere along the slash spectrum. Listening to their stories, I realized that people who have figured out how to add slashes to their lives are an incredibly fulfilled bunch, both in what they think of as work and what they think of as "life." What's more, they seem to have found the answers to some of the most vexing issues in working life today, from job insecurity to career burnout to work/life balance.

With this book, I hope to send many others down the slash path.

How to Use This Book

Think of this book as both a guide and a collection of inspiring stories. Part I introduces the kinds of people who develop slash careers and the many ways those careers tend to unfold. It begins with a look at the common characteristics and patterns of slashes.

Part II focuses on the practical aspects of creating and thriving in a slash life: how to best present yourself to others; how to benefit from the synergies of slashing; and how to overcome the particular challenges facing those of us who refuse to respond to the "What do you do?" question with a singular answer.

PART I

A SLASH CAREER: GETTING STARTED

Part I focuses on where people discover their slashes, the kinds of paths they travel while cultivating them, and how they figure out the places for their various slashes.

CHAPTER 1

THE SLASH MIND-SET: BEGIN, IMPROVE, REINVENT. REPEAT

I'm drawn to computer programming because it involves solving puzzles and the beautiful abstract understanding of complex things. It's what I spend a lot of my free time reading about. But after a while that work can feel arid, and I get really excited to get back to the theater where I work with people, telling stories, bouncing things around. But rehearsals are all vagueness and uncertainty, with all of these egos. And after a while of that, it becomes compelling to go back to a place where things are clean and simple. With the programming, even though I have collaborators and clients, in the end there's a sense that's just mine. There's something really nice about just solving a problem in my head that doesn't depend on if the paint color works, everyone remembers their lines, and the audiences like it. Basically, if I weren't doing both things, I'd get bored and antsy.

—Dan Milstein, computer programmer/
theater director

Dan Milstein, thirty-nine, moves between his work as a computer programmer and a theater director with elegance. By pursuing his multiple passions, his career nourishes him. But like most slashes, he has built his unique career over time, tweaking it as he goes along. When he spoke the words above, he was at a resting place, observing what was working to keep him *in balance* *for that moment in time.* Milstein's approach is an appealing way to think about a career, and about a life.

Milstein was always interested in lots of things. As a high school senior he took math classes at Princeton University at the same time as he edited his school's literary journal. When he arrived at Yale, he focused his coursework on math and computer science but gave all his free time to the theater. "Yale was the ideal creative home for me," he said, "the sort of place where all these high achievers would give thirty to forty hours a week above their coursework to some extracurricular activity. And the people who thrived were those who ran things on their own, which turned out to be perfect training for a life where no one gives you a job and tells you what to do."

He toyed with graduate school and was even offered a fellowship that would have paid for continuing his education in math and computers. But the computer department wasn't where his friends were, and such a focused course of study didn't seem like it would be satisfying. "It just didn't feel like a full life," he explained. Milstein also had a hunch that he might no longer be the star performer at the next level and that only the stars in academia had control over their lives. "I guess I didn't love it enough to think that I'd be satisfied doing the work if it meant living anywhere I was offered a job."

For several years after college, Milstein had a period you could easily refer to as floundering. He settled in Boston and got a job in a coffee shop, working the late afternoon shift so that he could devote the mornings to writing short stories. The writing didn't take off. "It was a period of lots of self-doubt," he said. "I wasn't sure if I could consider myself an artist, yet it was so compelling to me to be an artist."

Around the same time, he decided to use his computer background to get a day job that was more likely than his job at the coffee shop to pay off his student loans. He tried his hand at various jobs in the computer field and was disenchanted by a lot of what he saw—people who had become experts in doing one thing and were paid to do just that one thing, and jobs in tech support that weren't at all creative and where the staff looked universally unhappy.

Slowly, the tide began to change. It was the early nineties, the heyday of the dot-com boom, and programmers were sought after. Gig after gig materialized for Milstein, often through his coffee shop contacts. In one instance, he was literally hired off the street when he ran into a friend who brought him aboard a startup. "You know HTML. Come with me," was the basic pitch. Around the same time, Milstein abandoned his attempts to write fiction and turned his attention to the theater, from which he had drifted since his college days. Once he began directing plays, he knew he had found his creative home.

At his day jobs in the technology field, however, Milstein grew tired of worrying that his bosses would catch him on the phone stealing time to manage crises with the plays he was working on. He also realized he needed to work for and with people who valued the end result of what he did enough so that they didn't care how many hours he worked each day or where he did the work. Fortunately, work was so plentiful that Milstein realized he could be employed quite well without a "job." He partnered up with a buddy and began a consulting business.

Fast forward to today. He's working about thirty hours a week on programming (largely dedicated to a business he's helping to create) and up to sixty hours a week on Rough & Tumble, a theater company he founded—although the hours in any given week can vary wildly. The income split between the two hardly reflects the way he spends his time (he makes about $1,000 a year from his theater company and about fifty to a hundred times that from his consulting work). He identifies equally with each.

One of the reasons Milstein's setup works for him is that he is in control of both aspects of his life. In his artistic life he writes, directs, and produces what he likes to call "theater that doesn't suck." On the theory that theater should be accessible and fun, Rough & Tumble's plays involve physical comedy and often employ innovative approaches to language and expression. (One play I saw was an improvised Austin Powers–type caper in which "blah blah" was the only utterance by the actors—it was still possible to understand everything happening among the characters.)

Having two fully developed careers may sound like a recipe for workaholism, but Milstein is as passionate about his time off as he is about his twin vocations. For years, he took summers off to travel, and he's always made time for ultimate Frisbee and other hobbies. His philosophy is that being well-rested and well-rounded is part of what makes him excel at his jobs.

Milstein believes he wouldn't be a good fit for a client who would be impressed by how overworked he is. "There's a certain culture in programming where managers think they are doing a good job if everyone is working overtime," he said. "After being a programmer for ten years I've learned that is sort of a big lie. The most productive team is the one that closes down at five every day and has a clear head in the morning to see their way through problems. It's more like an art form than building a house. If you have a problem with a novel or a play, the solution isn't necessarily to write more pages. Often what you're doing when you're working on a novel or a play is looking for that burst of insight. And you won't get those unless you are fresh and unstressed."

Whether or not they are actual entrepreneurs like Milstein, serving as their own boss in their various endeavors, **most slashes show an entrepreneurial streak at the heart of their stories**. These are the kinds of people who are not satisfied to rest once they've achieved competence or milestones in a given field. They are inherently curious, eager to engage and immerse themselves in a multitude of areas. The notion of finishing up one thing and moving on to the next doesn't seem to exist for these folks. Instead, it's about building a complex identity, adding a new layer with each slash. Milstein's choice to abandon serious scholarship in computers is also emblematic of slash thinking; by keeping computers in his life in a less academic way, he was able to make room to pursue other things that are important to him. **Sometimes removing yourself from the fast track, or just slowing down a bit, is an ideal way to allow another passion or vocation to flourish.**

/ / /

Mary Mazzio, forty-four and an Olympic rower-turned-lawyer/filmmaker/mother, can't remember a time when she wasn't pursuing multiple interests at once. She attributes it to an unusually high energy level. "I was a slash to the tenth in high school and college and always wondered if that would lead to mediocrity," she explained in her signature rapid-fire speech. When she recited the list of activities she pursued in those years—ballet, elocution, cello, piano, tennis, swimming, "anything you can throw a lesson at"—she attributed it to her Italian-American dad and Irish-American mom: "They wanted to produce children with a higher pedigree, almost to an obsession." Mazzio didn't disappoint.

She went to law school directly after college, where she had dedicated a lot of time to rowing. During a semester in France, she joined a local boat club, and after law school, while working on successive fellowships in Yugoslavia and Korea, she found her way to rowing communities, training among (and often coaching) the best of each country's female rowers.

Back in Boston, Mazzio began to work as a real estate lawyer in a large firm. By then she knew she was a good enough rower that, with proper training, she could compete in the Olympics. She pursued both her legal career and the rowing (with a lot of support and accommodation from her law firm), and in the summer of 1992 she rowed in the Barcelona games. She didn't take home a medal, but that experience gave her the validation that she was a serious athlete, and it gave her a sense of commitment that has traveled with her in all her subsequent endeavors.

After the Olympics, Mazzio put aside the competitive oars, but the promise of a full-time legal career didn't appeal to her. "I was a lawyer, but I never thought of myself as only a lawyer, which seemed so narrowly defined," she told me. At the time, she was spending a lot of time on pro bono work, helping displaced tenants get their homes back. It was gratifying at first, but after a while she felt she was hearing the "same stories with different faces."

"I got so depressed, I just felt like I wasn't making a difference," she said. "That prompted me to think bigger, about how I could impact change on a larger scale. I had always been profoundly moved by film ever since I was a little girl. The power was so overwhelming in a way that made you think."

Within months of returning from Barcelona, Mazzio enrolled in an MFA program in film and began studying "on the sly," taking mostly evening classes or daytime classes during a time slot that could be disguised as a long lunch. (She feared that if the firm's partners knew she was studying film, they would question her commitment to the law and it might affect her chances of being promoted to partner.) "I had the best secretary at the time," Mazzio told me, switching to a working-class Boston accent. "'Mary is so busy,' she would say, protecting me from anyone who wanted to bother me."

She began writing screenplays with the goal of bringing new kinds of female characters to the screen. "I always thought the women in the movies didn't look like women I knew," she said. "They were gorgeous, but bland, insipid, and two-dimensional." Mazzio wanted to write about the women she knew, women who were "irritatingly smart," but who might have big thighs or be cranky with their periods from time to time—"basically real women with their whole range of characters and emotions."

Mazzio made some progress on the road to being a screenwriter. Several of her screenplays bounced around Hollywood and Mazzio had a series of meetings with the bigwigs. "All this stuff happened and then, in the end, nothing happened," she explained. "I kept feeling I was so close, but I wasn't really close at all." Concluding that the Hollywood odds were not in her favor, Mazzio took matters in her own hands. Ultimately, it was a true story—about a 1976 revolt by female rowers at Yale—that turned her into a filmmaker. She developed the idea in her classes, stepping up her work on it while home with her second child on maternity leave. "I was itching to get out of the house and those film classes were the perfect escape," she said.

Mazzio's legal background and connections came in handy during this period. Being a lawyer (and a female athlete) provided expertise in the film's subject matter, Title IX, the law enacted to bring equality to women's sports. And through her business relationships, she found both the technical experts and financial backers to get her film off the ground. **Using contacts and knowledge from one career to build another is a common slash technique.**

Having a supportive husband, who always encouraged her and who shared her philosophy on things like having a full-time nanny even when she was working part-time, was also very important to her being able to pursue her many passions. As she put it, "My husband knew I wasn't the type who'd have a home-cooked meal on the table every night."

Mazzio's maternity leave got her through preproduction on the film. By the time she returned to work, the film was in the middle of production. She had an inkling that her days as a lawyer were numbered. With two young children and two full-blown careers, Mazzio knew she was at the edge. "If I didn't make a change soon, something would suffer, not the least of which would have been my health."

Once the film was aired and press coverage began, Mazzio realized that she could resign from the law firm, the post she was holding on to to hedge her bets. As a filmmaker and a mother, she had as many slashes as she could handle, and because she runs her own production company she can control her schedule more than she could as a lawyer.

Leading a slash life often requires shedding a slash to make room for something new. For Mazzio, rowing and the law had run their respective courses, but each remains a fundamental part of who she is, as a mother, a filmmaker, and an entrepreneur. She's made films about athletes, mothers, the law, and even the intersection of these various themes. Her legal skills serve her well as a filmmaker.

/ / /

If Milstein and Mazzio represent the arrival at a destination, Jenny Vacchiano, thirty-five, is the embodiment of the journey. Writers and artists almost always have "that thing they do until they don't have to do it anymore." For Vacchiano, that thing was painting houses. I met her just at the moment when she was trying to wean herself from a fairly successful painting business she had built up. "I'm feeling kind of scared," she said several times during our conversation. The goal was to get the business down to half-time to make more room for writing. With several short stories published and a novel in the hands of an agent, she was moving in the right direction—if only the money gig weren't so consuming.

Vacchiano fell into painting houses her first summer after college when she moved to California and needed some steady income. Painting houses (interiors and exteriors) was easy, temporary work for someone still in the wandering stages of life. And for many years, through a master's program in Boston and even after graduate school, painting was the ideal side job. "I just love painting a room a color, a really bold color, and seeing the before and after. When you're working with your hands, your mind can just go," she explained. "And you're keeping your body in shape rather than sitting at a computer all day in an office and coming home to write on top of it." Plus, she was able to work for a few months straight—the spring through fall, when business was plentiful—and save up enough to spend the winter months on her writing.

Once she settled in Denver, the painting work became so steady that she started her own business rather than just taking jobs from other people. For a while, she enjoyed the entrepreneurial feeling of building something for herself. But soon, managing a business that was not her passion discouraged her. When business was good, she could be painting fifty hours a week, which left her physically tired. It was also hard for her to switch from the painting to writing mind-set within the same day. "If I was mid-project, it was disturbing to return after a week of painting to a day of writing. Sometimes it took me a whole day to remember where I left off and find my voice again. I just started to resent the painting. Writing gives me a purpose and to not do it, I'd think 'this is my life, this is it.'"

Vacchiano knew it was time to readjust, but readjustments don't happen overnight. When we last spoke, she was in the middle of the transition, hoping to set up a life with more slashes connected to writing. She'd made the decision to take on fewer clients, focusing on single rooms and jobs small enough that she could do them without hiring other people. To compensate, she was copyediting, getting her feet wet in freelance journalism, and stepping up her teaching commitments at the Lighthouse Writers Workshop, a writers' community in Denver.

Her life as a painter has seeped into her writing, though. On the day I first interviewed her, the *Denver Post* published an article Vacchiano had written about a professional color consultant whom she met through her business. She's even made one of the characters of her current novel a housepainter. "Camille works in a library and she's fed up with where she is. Sick of her boyfriend. Sick of her job. Sick of her life. She goes off to the shore, paints the house she's staying in, and gets a painting job with a crew of guys. She likes it, just like I did when I first started out," she explained, then added, "As for me, perhaps I'll work in a library like Camille did before she got hooked on house painting."

Though Vacchiano enjoys the painting work, she hopes to get to a point in life where she can give it up completely. She's comfortable with the idea of having slashes, but she would relish a life in which all her slashes could be connected to writing, like the teaching and freelance journalism work she's now pursuing. **It's all part of the constant tinkering that goes on in any kind of slash life.**

/ / /

Near the end of a group hike, a tour of an organic vegetable farm in Tecate, Mexico, I got into a conversation with Scott Sharkey, my guide. After a few hours of watching him, I thought I had him pegged. The ruddy-faced outdoorsman was all smiles and positive energy, awed and pleased by everything around him. Passing an open field, he pointed out a mama peacock protecting a new flock of chicks. On a dirt road, he shouted *Buenos dias* to the locals doing their brisk morning walks. I imagined he was in his late twenties, living in Mexico as a guide and fitness instructor at a local resort while figuring out what he would do with his life. As it turns out, he was in his mid-forties and for him, a life of wandering and using his talents for guiding and entertaining was an end in itself.

Growing up in Orange County, California, Sharkey knew he didn't want to end up like his father, who joined the navy to get an education, worked for one company his whole life, and, once married with children, fell into a routinized grind of work and home chores. Mowing the lawns on the weekends was his only brush with physical activity. Exercise was a memory of boot camp.

On graduating from high school, Sharkey seriously considered joining the police force, but after riding along with some middle-aged officers, he decided the men had no passion for what they did. He then focused on nurturing his talent for dancing and performing. In his twenties, he went to work for Disneyland, where his penchant for hamming it up with strangers made him a charismatic parade leader. Performing gave Sharkey a chance to travel—a stint in Okinawa, Japan, in the cast of a traveling musical; a sojourn in Argentina with another show; time in New York City, where steady work with flexible hours as a fitness instructor at high-end gyms allowed him time to pursue voice-over work and acting gigs. Ultimately, the combination of fitness training, leading hikes (like the one where I met him), and performing has allowed him to connect with people, remain youthful, and see the world. But recently he discovered he also has a knack for refurbishing real estate properties and selling them, a lucrative sideline.

For Sharkey, following his interests has led him to a place of balance—a life in which the journey and the destination are the same. He could never have planned the course he ended up on.

The notion that you can't plan everything is a hallmark of slash thinking.

/ / /

Carrie Lane, thirty-nine, a Pilates instructor/art consultant (and one of my oldest friends), is living proof of that. For most of her adult life, Lane followed a path that meshed with the expectations of her Ivy-educated peers. She studied art history as an undergraduate, took a series of internships and entry-level jobs at museums, and ultimately pursued a doctorate. Out in the world, she soon discovered a business opportunity in the large number of people who want to collect art but don't know where to begin. Thus was born Carolyn K. Lane & Associates, the consulting firm she founded with a twin mission: helping people make educated choices about art and helping up-and-coming artists find markets for their work.

Lane has always been athletic. Through high school and college she was a champion equestrian, competing in events on a national level. After a broken collarbone diminished her enthusiasm for riding, she turned to running, filling her free time with marathon training, scouting out races in other countries, and improving her finishing times. Next came mountain climbing. Then, a new form of fitness training, Pilates.

Like many people, Lane treated her work—the intellectual stuff she did with art—as distinct from her hobbies—those athletic pursuits that kept her fit and fueled her competitive spirit. People who knew her well often told her she would be a great trainer, but she felt she already had a career. With increasing frequency she started to wonder if it had to remain that way.

Around the time of the September 11 attacks, Lane was working with a private Pilates instructor; the exercises helped ground her in that time of turbulence. She was attracted to the theories behind Pilates, which uses specially designed pieces of equipment to increase core strength, enhance flexibility, and improve posture. One day it just hit her: coaching others in some kind of physical work had to become a part of her professional life. As she explained it, "With the art, I'm helping people and educating them. But I was feeling the intense need to help in a more hands-on kind of way."

The idea of putting her business on hold to develop a new slash was daunting, but she didn't overanalyze it. "I tend not to think too hard about things I want to do," she said. "I usually just move forward and then worry about how to deal with it later."

Becoming certified to teach Pilates is one of those immersion experiences, like basic training for the military or graduate school, when friends and family learn to do without you during your period of initiation. "During my training, I had to put everything, even a lot of my art stuff, on hold," she said. "I had to complete six hundred hours of training and wanted to do that quickly. Life was solidly Pilates for about six months."

Today, Lane is fully established in both vocations, with a part-time job at a health club, a small group of private Pilates clients, and her art business. She's busy, to be sure, but she rarely says no to an opportunity. In 2004, she was hired to write a scholarly book about the nineteenth-century American artist William Merritt Chase. That project, which occupies around twenty hours a week, will last for about three years. The challenge for Lane these days is deciding which of her slashes gets the most attention. "Sometimes I worry about spreading myself too thin, but it's cyclical," she explained. "When I have a new art client, my mind is preoccupied with art. But after a Pilates seminar, I'm reinvigorated by that and feeling more identified with my teaching. When I'm thick in the research for a Chase painting, the city

could be aflame around me, but I'm stuck in the 1880s, wondering about the identity of a mysterious figure in a painting."

Though Lane often feels pulled in many directions, each of
her vocations has benefited from the other. Many of her art
clients originally met her through Pilates and vice versa. "Often,
when a client in one work context hears about my other life,
they are curious and want to know more," she said. Synergies
like this are such a common part of slash life that an entire
chapter of this book (chapter 7) explores those issues further.

/ / /

One of the trickiest parts of writing a book about slash careers
is that often I'd check in with one of my subjects some time
after an interview only to learn that he or she had ramped up
one activity and scaled down another, or added an entirely new
slash to a seemingly full plate. Lapses of time could mean that
someone was finishing up a campaign to run for office, in graduate school getting an advanced degree, on sabbatical to write a
play, or taking a break from paid work to parent full-time.

**Thus, having a slash career requires being comfortable
with beginnings.** Sally Hogshead, a branding expert/author/
consultant, refers to this principle as being the "dumbest person
in the room." While nothing about Hogshead strikes me as
dumb, she told me that's exactly how she felt when she went
from high-flying creative director to fledgling author. "Nothing
was handed to me. In advertising, it had been years since I had
to make cold calls or explain why someone should hire me. But
I was back at level one. I had to earn my credibility from
scratch," she recalled. "I wrote a book proposal. People didn't
like it and it got rejected. They told me career books didn't
work like this. Anytime you're trying to add a new slash, before

you even start to dip a toe into that, you have to get comfortable with the idea that people may not think you should move into that area. I collected so much evidence that I shouldn't be an author. I'm sure anyone who's leapt into a new zone goes through that. That's innate to the process. I hired a writing coach to help me do the proposal. She said, 'You don't have this whole writing thing down. I don't think anyone will buy this book.' I had been making my living using my writing skills for over a dozen years and I had shelves full of awards telling me I was a good writer. Still, when my agent first saw it, it took weeks for him to call back and then weeks to even comment on it. I created proposals for a living at the top agency in my field and I went through a heart-wrenching year-long process."

We all have those moments of dumbness, as Hogshead calls them. They're the times of trying on new identities and navigating new worlds. Herminia Ibarra's book *Working Identity* distills the process people go through when they shed one identity and take on another in the process of career reinvention. She observes:

> Most people experience the transition to a new working life as a time of confusion, loss, insecurity and uncertainty. And this uncertain period lasts much longer than anyone imagines at the outset. An Ivy League Rolodex doesn't help; even ample financial reserves and great family support do not make the emotions any easier to bear. Much more than transferring to a similar job in a new company or industry or moving laterally into a different work function within a field we already know well, a true change of direction is always terrifying.[1]

Despite those feelings of "confusion, loss, insecurity and uncertainty," the only way people discover new identities is by facing down those feelings and moving past them. Marco Canora, a chef/restaurateur, talked to me about this when I met with him at his New York City restaurant Hearth in the summer of 2005. Canora was at a crucial point in his career, figuring out what to do next in a time when being a player on the restaurant scene seems to *require* the amassing of slashes.

Canora became known in foodie circles after he helped launch the successful restaurant chainlet Craft. But a good track record doesn't seem to be enough for someone to be considered one of the greats. Today, successful chefs are marketing empires, breaking out of the kitchen to build their brands by teaching cooking classes, writing cookbooks, and launching food-related product lines. Canora spoke candidly about the challenges of building a career in the age of celebrity chefdom.

To the outsider looking in, Canora was sitting in a coveted spot: he and his restaurant were attracting media attention at a steady pace; he had recently been invited to give master cooking classes in Melbourne, Australia; and he was being courted by agents for books and other media projects. In short, he was on the celebrity-chef fast track. Yet when we spoke, he was filled with apprehension. Restaurants thrive and die. There is pressure to open the next place, to expand the empire, to break into television and radio. "What if I make the wrong move?" he wondered aloud, in a moment of unguarded musing.

So many people avoid growing their careers for fear of being in just this place—giving up the known, the secure path, the steady income, the thing you know you're good at. The beauty of taking on a slash is that you can make a foray into new territory and still embrace the established career that gives you confidence, income, or whatever else it is that makes you want to continue doing it.

GETTING TO SLASH / / / / /

- An entrepreneurial streak is at the heart of most slash stories. Even if you work for someone else in some areas of your working life, building a slash career means you are taking charge of the mix of things you do.

- Sometimes taking yourself off the fast track in your primary career opens the door to building a second one. As an added benefit, you might avoid the burnout and narrowness of focus that often plague the highest achievers in a given field.

- Contacts and knowledge from one career can give you a leg up as you build another.

- Leading a slash life often requires shedding a slash to make room for something new; be prepared for a life of constant tinkering.

- Get comfortable with the idea that you can't plan everything.

- Synergies between various vocations are a common part of slash life; when they emerge, recognize the opportunities they afford.

- Embrace being a beginner. We are all insecure and filled with doubt when taking on new challenges. The only way to overcome those feelings is to acknowledge that they're part of the process and move past them. ■

CHAPTER 2 / SLASH BREEDING GROUNDS: STARTER PROFESSIONS, VOLUNTEERING, PASSIONS, AND DETOURS

I used to be a restaurateur. Now I'm a teacher. I'm a writer. I'm a mentor. I create. You work in a career, you focus solely on it, and all of a sudden you live and breathe one thing. It makes you a boring person. A lot of people think it's about either/or; I think it's about both/and.

—Alex von Bidder, managing partner of The Four Seasons Restaurant/yoga instructor/author/model

Career change used to be a cataclysmic event in a person's life. Now it's standard practice, something many people do, usually a few times, over the course of a working life. But this isn't a book on career change; it's a book that seeks to change the way you think about your career.

The major difference between changing careers and slashing is that slashes don't abandon their primary vocation. They enhance or reconfigure it, building on it or adding to it in some way. When they're done—if they can ever be said to be done—they end up with custom-blended careers.

One concern I often hear when talking to people about slash careers is, "It's hard enough building one career at a time. How do you expect people to build many at once?" My reply, inspired by a friend in the venture capital business, is to suggest thinking about your career in the way a venture capitalist thinks about her investment portfolio: **If you plant a lot of seeds, some will die and others will blossom into thriving plants.**

The same is true for the various slashes you cultivate in your life. This chapter will give you some ideas of where to find the seeds in the first place and how to determine if they're worth nurturing.

Springboarding from a Starter Profession

Everyone starts somewhere when building a career, and often those beginnings have something to do with their career path. Those foundational careers—or starter professions—are much like a starter home that helps you get to the next, more desirable one. They might be brief stints or long immersions, but whatever form they take, **starter professions can provide a foundation, a knowledge base, and a professional network, all things that are useful when reorienting a career.**

Unlike a starter home, however, a starter profession doesn't have to be left behind. Even if you modify the way you are involved in your starter profession as you take on slashes, often your background will inform your next move. In some instances, you might choose to retain your starter profession as you venture on to something new. Here's an example of how that's done.

Sanjay Gupta, the popular medical correspondent on CNN, was a neurosurgeon long before he found his way into television. It was his stature as a surgeon that made him qualified for his job in television—who better to advise American viewers on everything from how to avoid the flu to how to keep your weight down during the holidays than a real live physician? Viewers *believe* him because they know he's not just reading the news, he *understands* it. And with his friendly, upbeat demeanor, his bedside manner couldn't be better. Even more intriguing, he's still saving lives week after week in addition to delivering health news to his viewers.

How did he get there? I asked him this question during a telephone interview squeezed in between his reporting from Katrina-ravaged New Orleans and his vacation.

While still a medical resident at the University of Michigan, Gupta was selected to be a White House Fellow in the Clinton White House. The program, created by Lyndon Johnson in 1964, brings together people from different fields and gives them exposure to the workings of the federal government with the goal that the Fellows will return to the private sphere and contribute in some way to national affairs. Through the White House Fellows Association, Gupta met Tom Johnson, then CEO of CNN, who had been a Fellow some years earlier. The two of them had a lot of discussions about how healthcare information was being delivered by various news outlets. That relationship led to his current job at CNN.

Gupta's CNN post has him tackling stories that range from the offbeat—such as a series about the safety of NASCAR racing—to the superserious, like when he was stationed as an embedded correspondent with a U.S. naval unit in Iraq, where he performed brain surgery five times. His CNN gig could easily be full-time employment for someone else, yet Gupta continues to perform surgery, though on a much-reduced schedule. He says that working as both a correspondant and a surgeon actually makes him better at each.

When I talked to him in the fall of 2005, he was working about half-time in each of his endeavors, performing surgery on Mondays and every other Friday, and seeing patients on Wednesdays. At CNN, he has his own weekend morning show, *House Calls*. He's also a frequent guest on other CNN programs and is dispatched to cover medical situations around the globe. He says that his commitments to his patients come first, and if there is an emergency, he rearranges his television schedule. "In medical journalism, someone can usually step in," he explained.

Gupta doesn't view what he does as so unusual. In fact, he sees it as a return to a way of thinking that used to be common among doctors, before the pressure to hyperspecialize took over the profession. "I'm not that unique," Gupta told me. "Many doctors do and want to do other things. Years ago, it was commonplace that doctors were also good writers, interested in politics. That's just the way it used to be. We have become a more specialized society. This change didn't happen in a moment, but over a hundred years. And it happened because of insurance and regulations. Today, you're not only a doctor but you're a pediatric otorhinologist. You get accepted into medical school for your diverse interests and now, for the rest of your life, you'll focus on one small area. But putting blinders on is dangerous. What I'm doing is going from a microscope to a telescope."

A job as a neurosurgeon is not one many people would give up, so it's not surprising that Gupta has chosen to continue in it even as he's garnered the kind of celebrity only a few news anchors achieve. (His wedding was covered by *In Style* magazine, and he's been named one of *People* magazine's "Sexiest Men Alive." When I teased him about this last honor, he downplayed it. "That's just the power of television. When I lived in Michigan, no one other than my wife, then-fiancée, thought I was too sexy.") I believed him when he said he loved his work as a surgeon, but I couldn't help thinking he was also prudent to keep his hands literally on his scalpel. Television can be a fickle business.

Gupta, thirty-six, may be atypical in that his first career as a neurosurgeon puts him among the highest achievers of the workplace. But how many doctors, even among those with the intellectual heft to become surgeons, take advantage of a chance to embrace something new without giving up practicing medicine? Probably very few. "The hardest thing when doing something totally different is the risk. It's a gamble, in a way, when you are already well established in your field and successful" he says. "When doctors say 'I'll be on television once a week,' that's dabbling. When you say 'I'll move to a new town, cut my practice in half,' that is not."

Gupta says he doesn't feel like he's given up anything by adding a slash to his career, but he is more realistic about what he can accomplish. For example, before accepting the job at CNN he spent much more time on clinical research, but because he is affiliated with an academic hospital, he is still at the forefront of developments in his field. **Figuring out which parts of your job you can give up while remaining at the top of your game is an important step in making room for something new.**

Gupta is not alone in his desire to do more than what the traditional path seems to offer. His story is an example of the way opportunities present themselves when you amass knowledge and experience. And it is replicated often among people in all kinds of occupations.

/ / /

In the late 1990s, as a lawyer working part-time so that she could also care for her young children, Deborah Epstein Henry was feeling isolated and frustrated. She had a hunch that other women lawyers were struggling with the same issues affecting her: how to manage the daily logistics of their lives, the stigma against part-timers, law firms' dismal track records in promoting women, even disdain from stay-at-home mothers. So she sent out an e-mail to a handful of friends who also worked part-time asking if they'd like to get together to trade ideas about how to manage both work and family. About 150 responded.

Henry knew she was on to something. She began holding these meetings regularly, with the support of her law firm,

Schnader Harrison Segal & Lewis. In three years, those informal meetings turned into a business, Flex-Time Lawyers, which now has a mailing list of more than 1,600 lawyers in Henry's native New York and in Philadelphia. Henry runs her meetings like the Oprah of lawland, inspiring her members to negotiate for what they are worth and supplying them with the data and arguments to make persuasive cases for why law firms need to retain women lawyers.

Because she is in touch with so many lawyers, she knows their gripes and regularly plays the role of "Dear Debbie," giving out advice on everything from "what to do when you're called out of a deposition because your kid's stuck a bead up his nose" to "how to create some boundaries at work while still being thought of as a go-getter and team player." Law firms began to figure out that she was plugged in, and soon they started hiring her as a consultant on retaining and promoting women.

As Henry became recognized as an expert on work/life issues for lawyers, she collected more slashes. She now writes articles for magazines, and has become a popular public speaker. She has even started to dabble in recruiting. Recruiting wasn't something she really wanted to do, but after the umpteenth placement of a part-time lawyer looking for a job, she decided it was time to charge a fee for her time and effort.

For the first couple of years, Henry, now thirty-eight, kept practicing law for a few reasons. She needed the income while building her business. It also gave her credibility with the lawyers and law firms she worked with because she was still representing clients while dealing with the struggles facing her members. Eventually, Henry shifted her focus at her law firm, spending more time on business development and less on serving clients.

Staying connected to her law firm was a smart move for Henry, while also being good for her law firm. She gained credibility and the firm enjoyed the positive publicity her work generated. **The idea of keeping one foot in a starter profession to stay in touch with issues while launching a related venture is another common slash technique.**

/ / /

Robert Alper e-mailed me a few years ago after my first article about slash careers and introduced himself as a rabbi/stand-up comic. Over coffee, he told me his story, interspersed with one-liners. Billing himself as the "only practicing clergyman doing stand-up comedy . . . *intentionally*," Alper says he knew he was funny from the time he was two, when he made his older sister and her friends laugh with a pun that had something to do with the family code word for the posterior. "I can recall thinking, 'I'm one *funny* toddler,'" he beamed. As a teenager, he lived for the talent nights organized by his Jewish youth group. He memorized the routines of Bob Newhart and Shelly Berman, delivering them with little twists of his own to receptive crowds.

For years, though, being funny was a characteristic of Alper's personality rather than his career. After college, he followed his commitment to his faith and prepared to become a rabbi, studying for six years in the seminary and then earning a Doctor of Ministry at Princeton University. After years as a rabbi serving congregations, first in upstate New York and then in Philadelphia, he decided he wanted a life with more autonomy, so he left his congregation and opened a counseling practice. He also presided over "life-cycle events"—baby namings, weddings, and funerals—for unaffiliated people of any religion ("what we call hatching, matching, and dispatching," Alper told me, quickly adding that he can't take credit for coining that one). The counseling practice never got off the ground, but he quickly became busy with bookings for life-cycle events.

Just a few weeks after taking this new direction, Alper answered an ad in a Jewish newspaper to enter a Jewish comedy contest at a comedy club. The night arrived and Alper was nervous, but it was exhilarating to perform in a real club and in front of a receptive audience. That experience was enough to give him the confidence to seriously try his hand at stand-up comedy. Alper says a key ingredient to his transition was his wife, who worked full-time and is completely unmaterialistic; the couple eventually sold their house in Philadelphia and moved to Vermont, turning their vacation home into a full-time residence. Within four years, he was so busy with comedy gigs that he had to turn down wedding requests. "It was simply a matter of economics," he explained. Once in a while he still performs a wedding, but generally he leaves the weekends open for his comedy bookings.

Though Alper has largely given up being a traditional rabbi, he still presides over once-a-year High Holiday services at an independent congregation he convenes in Philadelphia. And his identity as a rabbi very much informs his act—he's the guy to call if you want humor that's "100% clean." It has also been his greatest marketing tool, since he's frequently booked for events at Jewish Community Centers and synagogues around the country. These days, he spends a lot of time touring college campuses with Ahmed Ahmed, a Muslim comedian from Los Angeles, in a performance billed as "One Jew. One Arab. One Stage. Two Very Funny Guys."

After our coffee, Alper sent me an essay written by Maurice Lamm, a well-known rabbi who left his congregation at age fifty-five to explore new vistas. This bit from Lamm's essay captures the essence of why many people feel the need to shake things up:

As a fledgling rabbi, I asked an old, recently widowed Russian Jewish butcher how life was with him. As he sat in the back of the empty store swigging a cheekful of hot soup and nibbling black bread, his answer was quick: "What is this life? Another pumpernickel. Another pumpernickel. Another pumpernickel." Is that what it's going to be for me at 55— just another pumpernickel?[1]

/ / /

In the previous examples, starter professions evolved naturally into slashes. Gupta, Henry, and Alper all found their slashes while doing the work they considered their primary professional identity. And in each case, their slash is related by content or subject matter to their initial career. In other instances, a starter profession helps you get to a place that is very different from your original work. In these cases, starter professions provide the economic security, confidence, or capital to explore something completely unrelated to a primary career. Aileen Bordman fits into this camp.

Bordman, forty-eight, has been a financial planner for more than twenty years. She finds her work gratifying and is extremely good at it, managing a portfolio of bonds worth over $100 million. I met Bordman through my cousin Marcia, who was one of her clients. "Bordman knows more about bonds than anyone," is the way Marcia, a savvy investor herself, described her.

Months after meeting Bordman, I noticed her name on the program of the Cape May NJ State Film Festival. I would not have been that surprised if she had been listed as a contributor, but she was listed as a filmmaker. I called my cousin in disbelief—"Your money manager is a filmmaker?" She confirmed it was true.

I met up with Bordman at the film festival, where her documentary, *Monet's Palate*, was being shown. After the screening of the film, she told me how she arrived at this place. "For some time I'd been feeling like my right and left brain were at battle," she explained. "My work was very gratifying, and not only from a financial point of view. Yet I was always passionate about the arts. I'm self-taught at guitar and piano and always had a passion for film. I was just not able to express that part of myself in the financial world. Some days I'd think the most visually creative thing I did in my work was decide what colors to use in a pie chart. Should the money market section be in fuchsia? Could I go that far?"

The urge to bring more creativity into her life continued to creep up. On a trip to France, that urge met up with an idea. While sitting at the dining room table at the estate in Giverny were the artist Claude Monet had lived and worked, Bordman was struck by what she called the "palette to palate" connection between Monet's appreciation for the colorful food of his native Normandy and his paintings. From that moment on, Bordman saw the concept as a film. She slowly shrunk her business down to a loyal collection of clients to make room for a new, and very consuming, project.

The film explores the relationship between Monet's art and the food of the Normandy region through cooking demonstrations with famous chefs and interviews with art collectors and scholars. From the start, Bordman conceived of the film not only as a piece of art, but also as a marketing vehicle for a line of products from the Normandy region of France. Being a complete novice meant figuring out how a film is made and financed and securing the participation of talents like Meryl Streep (who narrated part of the film) and casino mogul Steve Wynn (who went on camera to talk about his art collection) as well as the involvement of well-known chefs like Daniel Boulud and Alice Waters. She researched the trademark issues, prepared a Web site, and handled all of her own public relations. The skills and confidence she built up in her original business let her assume so many roles in the filmmaking process. "I think the fact that I was already a seasoned professional gave me the security to tackle something new and different," she said. "Had I tried to do this twenty years ago, without the business background, I would not have been able to do it. I was one of the first women bond traders on Wall Street. I think it all prepared me."

Bordman says that she made her film through sheer will and passion, along with some "direction from above," but with little formal training other than what she learned on the job. "I was a student of film as an observer from a very young age," she told me. "I would sit, eyes glued to the television, watching classic movies, and even at age twelve I would look at the lighting, and staging, everything about how they did this thing called film. I was mesmerized."

Through business, she knew the importance of finding the right partners. In the case of her film, her producing partner Steve, an entertainment lawyer, was a great help. "Steve has been around the filmmaking process for years as a lawyer," she explained. "Neither of us went to film school. We just learned the steps we needed to use our editing system, the sound, the camera, and lighting issues. He consulted with people about what kind of camera and editing system we should buy. In Steve, I also had someone to bounce ideas off of. Still, it was a first-time film for both of us, which means that many interviews couldn't be used because of poor sound or poor photography or both. With each interview, I got better. And with each phone call I made to cast the film or set up location shoots, it became easier and easier as I learned what to say or had the talent now connected to the project to help doors swing open faster."

Bordman's story teaches us a few things. First, her starter profession gave her the confidence to know that she

could make her film if she set her mind to it. Second, any new identity you take on is very much affected by where you come from. So many people have the creativity and inspiration for a film or other artistic creation, but they often lack the practical business skills that are necessary to pull it all together. When Bordman talked to me about making her film, she described it as if it were a business deal as much as an artistic creation. Managing a team of people, keeping to a schedule and budget, and arranging financing were all parts of the process, in which her professional background served her well.

Because Bordman was established in her money management business, she was able to figure out a way to keep that going even as she reduced the hours she spent on it. Thus, she could venture into something new without abandoning a career that still turned her on. Finally, the battle between her left and right brain arrived at a truce.

The next story shows another way an established career can be a help in acquiring a slash.

/ / /

On a spring day, with forsythia and cherry trees in bloom, I visited Robert Childs, a psychotherapist/violin maker, at his gray clapboard house in Cambridge, Massachusetts. At fifty-two, Childs has the enviable situation of moving between two workspaces within the confines of a private home. His three-story house is a fitting metaphor for the layers of Childs's life. The second floor, which holds a kitchen, bath, and study, is where his patients go when they arrive on a Tuesday or Thursday and take a seat on the leather chair for a session. On Mondays, Wednesdays, and Fridays, Childs heads up to the third floor, where he enjoys the quiet setting to make his instruments in a fully stocked woodshop overlooking the treetops. He even has a dress code for each vocation: jeans and a T-shirt or flannel shirt signal a woodworking day; slacks and a tie signal that he's planning to see patients. As we climb the stairs, he points out the paintings on the wall, all done by him.

Childs had an unusual career even before he acquired a slash—making violins the way people have made them for hundreds of years. He apprenticed for six years with two master craftsmen, first in his native Maine (where, he points out, having multiple jobs is a way of life) and later in Philadelphia. All along, he also played the fiddle, which he now does with Childsplay, a group of about two dozen fellow fiddlers who all play instruments made by Childs. His career in building instruments could easily support him in the lifestyle he enjoys. He makes about six instruments a year, selling each for about $15,000 to customers like Bonnie Bewick of the Boston Symphony Orchestra and Hanneke Cassell, a national Scottish fiddle champion. New customers wait at least a year for one of his custom-crafted pieces. As Childs told me about his passion for his craft and how he can even recognize the sound of one of his own instruments, I thought about how few people I've encountered who enjoy their work as much as he does. So why—at the height of his renown—did he add a completely new profession to his life?

In his thirties, Childs started to feel like he needed to make sense of his past—he was adopted as a child and never knew his biological parents. While he loved the parents who raised him, he spent some tumultuous years searching for his birth parents and began a course of intensive psychotherapy to work through his issues. During his therapy, he had a dream that he says helps explain what roles the violins and his therapy work would come to play in his life. In his dream, his search for his parents took him to the border of an unknown country. At the border, a guard took him into a quiet, windowless room where he discovered an engraved violin sitting on a table. The engraving was of a small boy crying. Childs's interpretation of the dream is that making violins gives voice to his childhood pain. "When I had that dream, I knew not only why I was a violin maker, but what was drawing me to psychology as well," he explained.

During Childs's training as a psychologist, his violin making supported him through eight years of clinical work and licensing. And as he built up his practice—he focuses on adoption issues, among other things—he saw no reason to give up his first love. He says the violins keep him grounded. "One of the dangers of psychotherapy is to end up living vicariously through your patients," he explained. "That really doesn't happen for me since I have a whole other vehicle for self-expression. Plus, I'd done this for thirty years and it takes so long to master a craft. My instruments are an artistic expression. Now that I'm here, I'd never give it up."

Like Bordman with her investment business, Childs used his violin making to support a foray into something new. But unlike career changers, these two had no desire to abandon their first careers. So many people reach a point in their careers—often around the ten-to-fifteen-year mark—when they realize there is a certain amount of repetition in their work (recall Rabbi Lamm's encounter with the butcher—"Another pumpernickel"). In some types of work, they also realize that what used to be challenging now comes with ease. These are some of the reasons why midlife career change is so common. **What people like Bordman and Childs realize is that leaving a career behind isn't the only way to reinvigorate after reaching a plateau; they instead choose to shake up a career by adding a new one, rather than replacing an old one.**

SLASH-IN-THE-MAKING /////

Marty Munson, forty-two and the health editor at *Marie Claire* magazine, has the kind of glamour job to which thousands of journalists aspire. With a lifelong interest in health and fitness, she is responsible for staying on top of health news and distilling it in an easy-breezy style that her magazine's readers want. Some perks of her job include: a trip to Italy to cover a conference on pasta; meetings with top medical researchers and nutritionists; and previews of new health-related projects.

Prior to her job at *Marie Claire*, Munson was a freelance journalist writing articles for a variety of health and fitness publications. It was one of those assignments that sparked her to pursue a slash. After working with a personal trainer for five weeks for a magazine article about the benefits of one-on-one training, Munson wondered how she'd be able to stay in shape once a magazine was no longer paying for weekly personal training sessions. Her conclusion: become a trainer herself. "I'd been around a lot of classes and a lot of gyms, but I wanted to be sure I was doing things right. Also, having studied dance in my twenties, I knew the importance of proper positioning and form. Basically, I got my certification because I wanted to know I was getting the 'official information' that would enable me to put together a smart cardio and resistance program for myself." But it wasn't just her own health she was thinking about. "I felt it would help my credibility as a health editor at a magazine to have an actual credential—in addition to all the medical studies I consume about exercise. Plus, I wanted to be able to help other people achieve their goals. Watching the New York marathon a few years ago and seeing those people meet or exceed their personal goals, I wanted to help people get to a place where their bodies could amaze them, whether that's walking five blocks, lifting thirty pounds, or doing a triathlon."

When Munson and I spoke for this book, she had just completed certification and was figuring out how to integrate seeing clients into an already hectic work schedule. Munson's magazine was supportive—even paying for some of the costs of training—and it's likely she'll get some exposure from time to time because her magazine is often called upon by other media outlets to give

expert advice on women's health issues. For now, she'll be satisfied taking on one or two clients—that's about all she'd have time
for in light of her job. By limiting her load, she has the benefit of
working with clients whom she feels she can really help, rather
than with anyone who comes her way. She is also being practical,
acknowledging that the magazine business is a tough one. "Training would also be a great way to take the financial pressure off if
I ever needed to freelance again—it would close the gap between
assignments and payment."

Sometimes slash careers are built by design, to plan ahead for
the types of careers—like in sports and the performing arts—
that are not known for respecting their elders. Early talent can
peter out. Tastes can change. Athletes can suffer career-ending
injuries. Even successful actors know that fame can be fleeting.
According to a *New York Times* article in September 2005, the
latest accessory for young actresses on the rise is a college
degree, something that will be useful when they make the
increasingly common move to writer/director/producer or
whatever slashes lie ahead:

> "The career life expectancy of an actress is pretty short," said
> Janice Min, the editor of *Us Weekly*. "It's still true that
> actresses over the age of 40 have an incredibly hard time get-
> ting good roles. If they go to college, the skills they learn can
> enhance their ability to write or produce or direct. It's almost
> like an investment, one of the better ones they can make."[2]

So many athletes and artists confront the realities when they
run into trouble. But like those young actresses returning to
school to get their degrees, cultivating slashes before you need
them can lead to a satisfying career even after the limelight has
dimmed. Case in point: Tim Green.

A former NFL football player for the Atlanta Falcons, Green, forty-one, divides his time between a law practice in upstate New York, writing books (several best-selling suspense novels, as well as two works of nonfiction), and radio and television commentating. Green obviously has some innate talents that have made a lot of his career possible, but after spending an afternoon with him, it was clear to me that there was also an awful lot of planning that went into building a life that allowed him to turn so many of his talents into professional paths.

I met with Green at a television studio in Secaucus, New Jersey, where *A Current Affair*, the tabloid news show he was working for at the time (he has since left the show), was being recorded. Though I'd seen him on television, he has the kind of shocking good looks that take a little while to get used to in person. But his comfort with all kinds of people and his ear-to-ear grin have a way of putting others at ease. Several times during our time together, people pulled me aside to tell me what a joy it was to have him around the station, mentioning the signed books he brought in for their parents or children, his interest in their careers, or the way he made others forget he's the celebrity in the room.

It's clear that humility and self-awareness played key roles in his success. Green worked on every strand of his current career during the period when most professional athletes are preoccupied with acquiring expensive toys and fighting off groupies. Always a family man, Green says he was not distracted by the usual pro-athlete temptations. Instead, he used the off-seasons of football to earn a law degree; it took him about eight years to make that happen. His writing flourished when he realized that football strategy meetings were an ideal time to jot down ideas that he would follow up on later.

By the time he retired from football after eight years of play, he had the makings of a new career. He knew that athletes get opportunities when they are at the top of their game, not later, so he took advantage of that by building his career as a sports commentator while he was still in the game. When he went into law, he managed to avoid the early years of grunt work that young lawyers usually endure in order to pay their dues. His work on the field allowed him to bypass these. "Most lawyers work for many years before they get to focus on rainmaking," Green told me, "but I did the inverse. I started out as a rain-maker and picked up my legal experience along the way." Today, he manages projects and interacts with clients. Because most male CEOs are eager for the chance to play golf or just converse with a former professional athlete, he knew he could bring value to a law firm.

In a sense, athletes have an advantage in that they know from the start that they will have to reinvent themselves when their bodies give out. If they are smart, they plan ahead. In Green's case, he realized that his time in the NFL was a prime period to begin developing the pursuits that would become his post-football career. During the years when he could have been collecting material possessions, he instead built some skills that would give him choices in the future. While he had early success as an author, he also knew that writing full-time was not something he could count on, yet another reason he pursued a law degree and worked on his television and radio career. This is a smart way to think even if you're not a professional athlete.

Having a slash in your back pocket—something you've been trained to do, something that gives you joy and pleasure—can be a wonderful luxury if your primary vocation turns out to be anything less than what you'd hoped for.

/ / /

Training "On the Side"

Todd Rosenzweig, a thirty-two-year-old marketing consultant in New York, is a happy-go-lucky guy who doesn't look like he works too hard to be that way. Jobs came naturally as he moved from one business opportunity to the next. His charisma and smarts made him a natural marketer. When I spoke to him, he had been working for several years in public relations for a small financial services business he respects. He was making a good salary and had been given a piece of the business. A lenient work atmosphere meant that he traveled often and could work at home a few days a week. But soon into our conversation he voiced a refrain that's common among people seeking to shake up a career. "It's not my passion in life. It's their passion, their company," Rosenzweig said. "My job is very interesting. And I'm motivated to see this business grow and do well. It's on the cusp of taking off. And I've worked hard to get here, so I don't want to leave right now. But . . ."

The "but" Rosenzweig got to is one I've heard so many times: "*But something else showed up in my life that felt more like a passion, a calling, a thing I just* had *to do.*" In Rosenzweig's case, the thing that arrived was a desire to learn about cutting-edge theories of nutrition and holistic health. His sister's friend had recently become a certified holistic health counselor and he was intrigued whenever she talked about that program. In many ways, he felt his life had been preparing him for this point. "I've always known about the need to eat right and how fucked up our society is in pushing food that's not really food," he said. "Even as a kid I knew an Oreo wasn't really food. A year ago I started eating more fruits and vegetables every day, drinking more water. I was always getting sick. Now I have a lot more energy. I accomplish more. I saw the direct result of treating my body better."

SLASH TIP / / / / /

Todd Rosenzweig is learning the way so many slashes do it—using scraps of free time to immerse himself in something new without leaving an existing job. Slashes like him take advantage of executive education programs and earn MBAs or MFA degrees on a part-time basis. Often, if their primary careers already involved advance degrees and years of study, their slashes are acquired through immersion experiences like culinary schools or adult internship programs a la Vocation Vacations, a company that lets you "test drive your dream job" by spending a vacation trying out life as a dog trainer, auctioneer, or private investigator. They log on to their computers for distance learning programs, take workshops to improve their writing or public speaking skills, or get certified to become life coaches, real estate brokers, Reiki instructors, or nutritionists. Most often, they learn by doing.

In pretty short order, he plunked down $8,000 and signed up to do the same program his sister's friend had completed. Rosenzweig is still not too sure what he'll do when he finishes, but he's already gotten his first three clients, one of them his boss. "I'm setting myself up to follow a passion into the future," he explained. In the present, Rosenzweig will be giving up a lot of weekends and evenings to study and get the most out of his program.

Passions, Hobbies, and Detours

Jamie Donegan, forty-six, is an actor/director who's proud to say he never waited tables. After studying performance and theater at Indiana University, he decided he was ready for New York City. At twenty-two, he packed up the proverbial van, drove east, arrived, and did what every young actor does: got two jobs—one answering phones, the other in a restaurant. He then went back to his apartment and felt depressed. That same day the phone rang and he got an offer to go on the road with a company that produced musical variety shows used as charity fundraisers. He had applied for the job months before on the recommendation of a friend but had forgotten about it.

Donegan accepted immediately and began a life of traveling from small town to small town, writing, casting, and directing shows. He has been producing these shows—first as an employee for a series of production companies and then for a firm he owns—for about twenty years. Though he never made it to Broadway, he doesn't regret his choice because it has given him creativity and security, a winning combination for any performer. And it has an added perk: it's seasonal, leaving summers free. In the early part of his career that seasonality allowed him to indulge his wanderlust. "That's when I'd take all the money I'd made and travel around Europe and blow everything I had," he explained.

Once he settled into domesticity, with a house and yard in Philadelphia, the off-season became a time for his hobby—gardening. He offered his services to an old estate near his home that was falling into disrepair. As his handiwork blossomed, he became known by the wealthy Main Line women who worked there as docents. Little by little, they started asking if he was available to landscape their gardens. Soon a business was born and he began doing for a fee what he had been doing for free. **Basically, Donegan created an "adult internship," a way to sample a new vocation, hone his skills, and make contacts in a new field. And like any good internship, it led to a real career.**

Landscaping was the perfect seasonal complement to Donegan's theatrical life, and it created other kinds of benefits too, as

SLASH TIP /////

Just as so many people discover their first careers by looking to their hobbies, so many slash careers develop that way too. But unlike trying to turn a hobby into a primary career, if you're just turning something into a side gig, suddenly the pressure to succeed is off. You already have a career so there is a lot less to lose. It's almost like the old saw in dating—you find someone when you're not looking. Another benefit of turning a hobby into an income-generating sideline is that the satisfaction you get from the activity is less likely to dissipate because you do not have the financial pressure of doing it full-time.

he explained to me. "As a Gemini, the two careers have given me balance. Just when I'm sick to death of listening to all of the questions and egos of my production gig, I get to go play in the mud in someone's backyard. On the flipside, just when I'm sick of manual labor and the toil in the soil, I get to go play dress up with people and make magic."

/ / /

Michael Melcher has had a series of what he calls professional "labels"—as an entrepreneur, a lawyer, a diplomat in the Foreign Service, and, most recently, as a career coach/writer/ speaker. But it was his early interlude as an accidental novelist that helped him figure out a fundamental part of his career vision. In the late 1990s, a few years out of college, Melcher and three classmates from Harvard collectively wrote a novel, *The Student Body*, inspired by a prostitution scandal that took place at nearby Brown University during their college years.

Over a period of five years, the group wrote as a team, bunking together in apartments and in borrowed houses for intense writing sessions. When they were apart, they used conference calls, group e-mails, and computer file round-robins. The idea is credited to Melcher, but the group claims equal ownership of the book. Melcher says the experience gave him a new way of looking at himself. "Writing that novel was a highly definitional experience for me. It's how I started to change my core identity from professional person to creative person. Yet oddly, I didn't think of myself as a writer until years after the book was published. I didn't think it really 'counted' because I wasn't like the other people I knew who thought of themselves as writers."

By chasing a dream—even one as seemingly far-fetched as co-writing an era-defining novel with three friends—Melcher learned something very important about himself. He learned that whatever he did in his career had to involve some amount of creativity. The fact that his experiment was successful gave him confidence about his ideas and made it easier to take other risks in his professional life. Most important, he had a good time in the process. Following your interests usually leads to an appealing destination.

Does It Have to Produce Income?

Whenever I talk about the slash concept, people invariably ask me whether a slash has to earn money to "qualify." Why is it that we call something a career or vocation only if it provides us with income, when very often the things that define us most, the things we answer with when people ask us who we are and what we do, are not just the things that pay the bills? Is Dan Milstein, from the beginning of chapter 1, any less an actor/director because he supports himself with his programming work?

Joseph Weilgus, twenty-eight, founded Project Sunshine, a nonprofit organization that provides resources to children with severe illnesses and their families, well before he even had a paying job. As an undergraduate at Yeshiva University in New York, Weilgus started spending time in local hospitals, where he would visit sick children. He noticed that many of them were alone and awake in the evening hours. "How do you not want to spend time with the fourth child of a single mom splitting her time between the hospital and the other three at home?" he asked me, implying that anyone would have thought to do what he did. One day, on a lark, he put on a clown costume, and soon he was "booked" by kids who were requesting visits. Weilgus started recruiting friends and classmates to join him in "spreading the sunshine" in any way they could think of, and before long, he was basically running a matchmaking service out of his dorm room between volunteers and local hospitals. Within a year, he'd amassed more than a hundred volunteers. By the next year, the number exceeded a thousand.

Meanwhile, Weilgus graduated and started out doing tax audits at PricewaterhouseCoopers. Within a few years, he jumped to American Express, where he focused on structuring business deals for institutional and individual clients. Then on to Geller Holdings for more of the same. But he never gave up on Project Sunshine, giving all his free time to recruiting volunteers, raising money, getting press, and doing whatever else the organization needed. In 2002, Weilgus was named Nonprofit Entrepreneur of the Year by Harvard Business School. By the time Project Sunshine received a grant that would allow it to bring on some paid management, everyone looked directly at Weilgus. He flatly refused, explaining that he could do more for the organization by continuing his climb in the world of money, where he's somewhat of a missionary for directing prominent people and their money toward Project Sunshine. "It was clear I could do more for Project Sunshine by hiring someone else for that job," he told me. "The more influential I've become, the more people I've been able to involve at a higher level. Plus, I'm about giving money to Project Sunshine, not taking it."

Running a nonprofit organization as large as Project Sunshine is clearly something that would qualify as a career for someone. And for the full-time staff of seven that Project Sunshine employs today, working there is their job. Weilgus figured out what made sense for him. **The place that something occupies in your life—the paycheck, the gratifier, the giveback, the passion—is all up to you. In a slash career, you can control what goes where.**

/ / /

I met David Jonker a few years ago at a party in Connecticut that was filled with lawyer and banker types. I'm not sure which he told me first—that he was a banker by day or that he was captain of his town's volunteer fire department—but I know that all we talked about was his firefighting, which was the source of his greatest pride. It was also pretty clear to me that it was work, even if he never got paid for it.

Jonker, who is forty-five, has been involved with firefighting his whole life, but unlike the firemen who learn the ropes from their fathers, he fell into it during college when he was trained as an EMT and joined the volunteer fire department. Just like those who inherited the job, Jonker caught the bug. He says that firefighting is the ultimate challenge, when you risk your life to save someone else's house or property. "It's about situations that would make other people's hair crawl. You don't know what to expect when you get there. Four of your five senses are muted. You have no sense of sight in smoke-filled rooms. You have no sense of touch because you're encapsulated in that suit. You have no sense of smell or taste because of the air mask. You only have your hearing. Your job is to find the fire and put it out."

So why not do it full-time? I asked him.

"Money is an issue and I like New Canaan, an expensive place to live," he said. "The firefighting as a volunteer lets me have the quality of life I enjoy. I have everything." In fact, when he and his wife were deciding on where to live, they settled on New Canaan, Connecticut, in part because its fire department had room for both full-time and volunteer members.

Jonker reminded me of Mike Safris, my mother's longstanding accountant, whom I've known since I was a kid. Safris, who is sixty, has been a CPA for thirty-five years. As a young man, he toyed with the idea of joining the police force, but as he put it, "It's not something my overprotective Jewish mother could handle."

He forged ahead as an accountant, earning a comfortable living and riding a motorcycle to feed his hunger for a little adventure. When he learned about the possibility of serving as a deputy sheriff, a volunteer position in his local police department, he realized that there was a way to do police work as a complement to his life, rather than as a primary career.

"I like people and with this work I'm out in the community, working the fairs and carnivals, church functions," Safris said. "Little kids want to jump on my motorcycle. I don't do it because it's a way to 'give back'—it's not like I'm going to nursing homes, though I'm sure people get the same feeling from that. Two months ago a woman was beaten up in a park and we responded. We didn't know if she was dead or alive. We were able to activate EMS and we brought her to the hospital. I'm not even sure that we saved her, but we felt good. I sometimes wonder how it would have been had I done this full-time. I think maybe I wouldn't feel the same way. Maybe I'd be burned out by now. For regular police officers, they are dealing with the same situations every day, risking their lives. I can't imagine where I'd be, to tell you the truth."

For both Jonker and Safris, protecting their communities made more sense as a volunteer activity than as a career. Both preferred to pursue careers that were more lucrative. Safris says he plans to step up his commitment to the police work when he retires from accounting. **Different life stages are often natural times to revisit the places slashes occupy in your life.**

/ / /

In January 2002, Roald Hoffmann, a Nobel Prize–winning chemist/poet/playwright, launched what he calls the "Entertaining Science Cabaret" at the Cornelia Street Café in Greenwich Village, New York. Since then, once a month on Sunday evenings, he's the emcee of a gathering that celebrates the intersection of things scientific and literary.

Hoffmann, sixty-eight, says he is trying to bring a little science to the cafe scene. "The performers in the series juxtapose science with music, the written and spoken word, art and performance," he told me. "When it works, science emerges as human, lively, and fun. One came from knowing Kenny Greenberg, a successful maker of neon lights for Broadway productions. I asked him if he would design something for our little stage. And I suggested he include a dancer I knew, Rachel Cohen, as a way of 'animating' the lights. He in turn introduced me to Clare Brew, a light artist. The three of them came up with two wonderful pieces; in one of them the dancer affected sensors that controlled the lights. I came into the show (I usually don't) talking about light and spectra—we gave out diffraction glasses to everyone in the audience. And Oliver Sacks talked about the discovery of the noble gases, a favorite subject of his."

When I interviewed Hoffmann, I knew of his reputation as a chemist and scholar. I had heard that he "also did some writing." I had no idea that "some writing" meant three volumes of published poetry, numerous essays, a play (broadcast by the BBC and staged around the world)—all in addition to the scores of books and scholarly articles he writes about chemistry, his major field of expertise. Hoffmann, who did not start writing until he was in his forties, said it was poetry that first sparked his literary muse. He says that writing poetry is a way for him to express things he could not express through science. "In poetry ambiguity was of value—that a word means three things and sounds like ten other words, that's poetry. Ambiguity has no value in science."

Sometimes you just have something you need to express, something that doesn't seem to have a place in the other corners of your life. Or something for which the usual language you work with doesn't provide the right voice. When you do, why not find a positive outlet for it?

GETTING TO SLASH / / / / /

- If you plant a lot of seeds, some will die and some will blossom into thriving plants. The same is true for the various slashes you cultivate in your life.

- Don't discount the value of your starter profession. Starter professions can provide a foundation, a knowledge base, and a professional network, all things that are useful when reorienting a career.

- Taking on a slash—or exploring your field from a different perch—can make you better at your original work.

- Figuring out which parts of your job you can give up while remaining at the top of your game is an important step in making room for something new.

- When launching a slash that's related to your original field, make sure to keep one foot in your old world. It will keep you connected to the issues and enhance your credibility as people learn about your new line of work.

- Any new identity you take on will likely be affected by where you came from, which means that you will bring skills and perspective that set you apart from others.

- So many people reach a point in their careers when they realize there is a certain amount of repetition and lack of challenge in their work. Adding a slash can be a terrific way to revitalize a primary career.

- Having a slash in your back pocket—something you've been trained to do, something that gives you joy and pleasure— can be a wonderful luxury if your primary vocation turns out to be anything less than what you'd hoped for.

- Take advantage of the countless ways to try out something new without leaving your current job. Identify the pockets of free time you have—whether it's weekends, evenings, summers—and enroll in a course, start a training program, or sample a new vocation.

- Consider creating an "adult internship," a way to expose yourself to something new or test out a hobby as a career path. Offer your services to an organization that needs your skills or where you can get training and exposure, and begin to build a network.

- Different life stages are often natural times to revisit the places slashes occupy in your life.

- When you try to turn a hobby into a full-time career, there is a lot of pressure to succeed. Instead, if you take it on as a slash, the pressure to succeed is off. You already have a career, so there's a lot less to lose.

- The place that something occupies in your life—the paycheck, the gratifier, the give-back, the passion—is all up to you. In a slash career, you can control what goes where. ■

CHAPTER 3

THINKING LIKE A MODERN MOONLIGHTER

Traditionally, moonlighting was something you did when you were short on money and needed to meet the monthly bill cycle. My experience is that now it is the very well educated and very secure people who are in the best position to be able to do multiple things because we're the ones with access to the technology and support to do one job flexibly while having time for another passion.

—Karl Hampe, management consultant/
aspiring cartoonist

Ruth Roche, my hair stylist, was showing off her rather buff arms while cutting my hair one afternoon. When I asked how she stayed in such good shape, she told me she worked with Oscar Smith, a personal trainer who owned a one-on-one training studio around the corner from her salon in New York's Tribeca neighborhood. Roche said the most intriguing thing about Smith was that he had a "whole other life," working the night shift as a narcotics officer.

What intrigued me most is that his personal training is the slash that came first. Police officers commonly have other jobs, but usually they fit an extra-money gig around their work in law enforcement. Smith, cop by night and trainer of Victoria's Secret models by day, has flipped that notion on its head. I had to meet him.

I interviewed Smith at O-Diesel, the sleek studio where he trains his supermodel and CEO clientele. As we talked, with a waif warming up on the stationary bike nearby, he explained that his job with the police department was the perfect way to build up his credit in order to get financing for his personal training business.

Smith joined the police force at twenty-nine. If he sticks it out, he'll qualify for a pension and retire by the age of forty-nine, practically mid-career by today's standards. Rather than taking on a job just for the money, Smith chose something that would feed his desire to help people and serve the community. Smith had worked as an ocean lifeguard since he was in high school and had saved thirteen lives over the years; protecting people from danger as a police officer was something he knew he would like.

Not everyone could do what Smith does. Working an evening shift that lasts from 3:00 to 11:30 p.m. and then training his clients in the early morning hours at his studio gives him very little sleep during the week. Still, Smith said it works for him because he takes good care of himself and reaps the benefits of working in two occupations that give him different kinds of satisfaction. I couldn't help noticing that he looked completely rested and relaxed. His tanned and toned body didn't show any signs of overwork, and I believed him when he told me he's caring for his body even as his sleeping habits violate every health rule in the book. It helps that he's a gifted napper. He returns home to catch up on sleep whenever a client cancels or he has a two-hour open slot, which happens often for personal trainers.

For Smith it was all about finding a job that he felt good about doing, as well as something that would give him the security to take on the risk of a business. Smith was used to putting in grueling hours, so for him, the relatively cushy schedule of a civil servant feels almost part-time. Shifts are eight hours long, but by tacking on an extra thirty-five minutes a day, he earns an extra day off each month. Add those twelve days to the eighteen he's already got coming and that's five weeks of paid vacation. All the more time for O-Diesel. His combination may not make sense for anyone else, but all that matters is that it works for him. For this point in time.

/ / /

The prior chapters focused on building slash careers to cultivate passions or make room for competing interests, but that isn't the only reason people have slash careers. Many people take on a slash to provide extra income or security while chasing a dream, pursuing a creative endeavor, or working in a low-paying but rewarding field. These folks are different from the moon-lighters of earlier generations. Forget cobbling together dreary day jobs or night jobs to make some extra bucks; today's moon-lighter shops for the perfect slash (or collection of slashes) that best accommodates the passion that occupies first place.

With actors, writers, and entrepreneurs earning steady income working as lawyers, real estate agents, or Web site developers, it's getting harder to tell the difference between a day job and a dream job. Smith chose one path, a job with secu-rity to complement the risk of his business, but many modern moonlighters are drawn to work that can be done flexibly or remotely. Or work that gives them wide open swaths of time to work on their own projects.

These folks say they know what comes first. But sometimes what begins as a money gig evolves into a full-blown second career. This chapter will look at the many ways people are thinking creatively about finding an ideal money gig to complement a passion or high-risk venture.

/ / /

When Sarah Graham, thirty, decided to become a journalist, she knew she was entering a field notorious for its low pay. While she was finishing up journalism school, she took the advice of one of her professors and picked up a skill—Web site design—that would give her a way to make some extra cash on the side. That professor, Sreenath Sreenivasan, who teaches new media journalism and is a general journalism gadfly, was also responsible for supplying Sarah with a bevy of journalists and authors who were eager to have her build their Web sites. When she began her consulting business, she hadn't even secured a job in journalism; for a few months Web design was her full-time job. But once Graham got a job as editor for the online branch of *Scientific American* magazine, Web design moved to second position.

Even with a solid journalism job, the extra income has made a big difference to Graham. "Living in New York is painful. While I could live on my salary, I just wouldn't be saving any money," she explained. "With this, I can basically do it on the side and it's almost one hundred percent savings."

I've been Graham's client since I launched my own Web site (or more precisely, since Graham launched it for me) a few years ago. And though I always knew she had another life, she rarely talked about it. We communicated only by e-mail and I knew that even if I never heard from her during business hours, once an evening had passed (and she had been home), the changes to my Web site would miraculously appear. To my mind, she had discovered the perfect slash to complement her job. **Her Web work is virtual, portable, and flexible, a desirable triumvirate for any slash**; and even though she started it up to make extra money, she's discovered that she enjoys it. "I get to use a different part of my brain. It's sort of like people who tinker in their tool shed on the weekend. It feels kind of like that because you're making something. And one of the best things," she said, "is that you never get production block the way you get writers block."

Graham's sideline works for some other reasons as well. **Because she's an entrepreneur with a Web business, the business gives her a sense of autonomy and control often missing from a job.** She has also built up some technical skills in her business that have helped in her career. Recently Graham took a new position at the *New York Times*. When she made that move, it turns out that the experience she brought from her Web business was just as valuable as the skills from her editing job. When I last spoke to her, she was steeped in the learning-curve phase of a new job, putting in long hours, and therefore not so interested in bringing on new clients. But she says there is no reason to give up the business.

If Graham experienced the side gig as a pleasant surprise, Ann Guttman won the modern moonlighting jackpot. Guttman, a professional musician, got into selling real estate as the proverbial backup. By her mid-twenties, Guttman, now fifty-one, was at the top of her game as a performer. She was playing her French horn regularly with the New York Philharmonic, the Long Island Philharmonic, and in the pits of Broadway musicals. At about the same time, a musician friend with a touch of the pragmatic began to rib her: "Look around. See any women in their fifties doing this? And if you do, do we want to be them, schlepping our instruments from gig to gig?" That teasing, coupled with the low periods of waiting between those prestigious freelance jobs, made Guttman wonder if it might be wise to nurture another career alongside her music.

Following the advice of all career experts, she looked to her interests. She was president of the board of the apartment building where she lived and decided that dabbling in real estate sales might suit her. Nearly twenty years later, her real estate career is as much her identity as her music. Initially, she always said she was a musician when she met new people, but over time that changed. She now relishes her role as a senior manager in a large real estate firm, mentoring the younger associates and enjoying the thrills of helping people find the perfect home.

Just two years ago, her life took a sudden twist when she contracted focal dystonia, a debilitating illness that often strikes musicians and others who overuse certain muscles. Guttman went through an excruciating period, dealing with both the pain of the disease and the emotional turmoil of retiring as a musician. Then, just around the time she was coming to terms with that, she was given a promotion at Coldwell Banker, where she now manages one of its busiest offices. "I feel so lucky. At a stage of life where I could be mourning this loss, I don't just have a fallback job, I have a career I love," she told me.

Guttman's experience shows that while **you can never know when a job will turn into much more than that, you can stack the odds in your favor.** Guttman didn't become a real estate agent solely for the promise of a good income. She chose it because she loved talking real estate, meeting new people, and getting the chance to visit all kinds of living spaces. This kind of self-awareness usually leads to smart career choices. But so many people don't bother with that kind of thinking when they are focusing on how to pay the mortgage.

Guttman isn't the only performer who's figured out that real estate is a very slash-friendly sideline. In New York City, where she lives, real estate has been touted as the "new waiting tables" for some time. This quote from an article in the *New York Times* makes light of the ubiquity of the actor/Realtor combination:

> In this city's central casting office, few stock characters are more set in their roles than the slick and savvy real estate agent and the starry-eyed starving artist waiting tables. But increasingly, the two high-risk, high-gain professions are becoming a mutually beneficial hybrid. The real estate agent at the open house may have a familiar voice because he was selling shampoo on television the night before.[2]

The article goes on to explain the reasons that actors are drawn to real estate brokering: flexible hours; a low barrier to entry (taking a brief course and passing a licensing test is usually all it takes); and the appeal of a professional rather than service-oriented job, among others. The phenomenon isn't limited to performers. Entrepreneurs are also widely represented in the ranks of part-time brokers, as are parents looking to keep their fingers in the work world during a period of hovering near home.

Working as an agent is only one avenue in real estate. Investing or refurbishing properties, becoming a landlord, or even running an inn or hotel are other ways that slashes use real estate to complement other pursuits.

Robert Sudaley, forty-four, has been an earth science teacher in middle school for more than twenty years. He became a teacher out of a desire to share his passion for education, but over the years his enthusiasm waned as he became frustrated by the aggressiveness of parents and the pressure to assign higher grades. Still, early on he realized that teaching was a career with a lot of tradeoffs. "Teachers may not make a lot of money," he told me, "but the structure of the job affords a lot of opportunities because (1) you work limited hours; (2) you have summers available to do other work; and (3) you have a guaranteed annual pay increase as well as a secure income, which is attractive to lenders." In his early years as a teacher, Sudaley enjoyed the hours and lifestyle of the teaching life. He stayed after school coaching the volleyball team and tutoring students in math and science, all of which came easily to him and brought in some extra income. During summers, he worked as a leader on cross-country bus trips, getting paid while touring the United States. After about a decade of teaching, he started to understand the economic value of the third point—the benefit of having a guaranteed income when buying property.

Sudaley lives on Long Island, New York, and in the summers he would drive around the Hamptons looking at houses. He already owned a house in Huntington, near his school, but he wanted to own a second home near the beach. Everything he looked at was beyond his reach, until he decided that he would buy a plot of land and try to build a house on his own. Sudaley isn't an architect or a builder, but he knew he was good with numbers and following a budget, so he hired a builder and went ahead. When the house was completed the builder happened to need a place to live for a while, so Sudaley rented it to him. The next summer, he had another tenant. All along, Sudaley was watching the housing market rise. He sold that house after the second summer season and used the proceeds to get to work on another house.

Managing his properties soon consumed more and more of his time. Since school let out at 3:00 p.m. (and he had given up all after-school activities), he was able to focus on his real estate projects in the afternoons; he also could work full-time during vacations and summer months. As his own boss, he scheduled meetings with banks and lawyers around his teaching job. And then finally, in the year I met with him—the seventh of his slash arrangement—he had decided to take a one-year leave of absence because his business grew so big that it needed all of his time.

I asked him whether it was hard to be his own boss in one corner of his life while adhering to very strict rules in another, wondering if that shift was a difficult one to manage. "I'm so used to the rules I'm supposed to work under as a teacher," he explained. "I just know what's expected of me. But my success outside of school has empowered me within the school. When I sit down with parents, during union negotiations, in whatever context, I talk from a position of strength. It allows me to say things that other teachers often won't say, things people are afraid to say. I teach in an affluent community and as homes go up in value to millions of dollars, I'm willing to fight for our raises. I've learned that if you don't stand up people will walk all over you."

Sudaley says his experience as a builder has increased his confidence in addition to expanding his bank account. He now wants to teach others how to follow his lead. Sudaley believes so strongly in the idea that all teachers (and other civil servants) should supplement their income by investing in real estate that he has self-published his book, *Financial Wellness for Teachers*, explaining his philosophy. Sudaley plans to be the pied piper of teacher slashes.

Sudaley's story is interesting from the flipside as well. Teaching, in its many forms, is about as slash-friendly work as you can find. In Sudaley's case, teaching was his starter profession. The security and steady income from teaching allowed him to develop his real estate investments. But just as often, people come to teaching as a part-time post to complement something else they are doing.

/ / /

Sometimes, the ideal slash isn't just one activity, but rather a collection of them. Victoria Matlock, twenty-seven, left Salt Lake City to try to make it in New York as an actor and has been working on building up a few businesses to offset the uncertainties of an acting career. Even though Matlock has had some early signs of acting success, she says she was raised to think about her fallback options. So, she followed her father's advice and majored in computer science. Now she's grateful she has the degree because it has allowed her to bypass the restaurant work route that she says she isn't cut out for.

Her computer background led to her first slash—building Web sites for actors and others in the theater community. In addition, she works as a photographer, specializing in actor headshots. She's also started to design a line of handmade purses, which she sells through her personal Web site. Matlock has been able to support herself through these budding businesses for the past few years. Equally important, she enjoys everything she does. In fact, she told me that if she died tomorrow, she'd be content with what she's achieved. That's a big declaration for an actor on the rise in the most competitive city in the world.

A key ingredient in Matlock's happiness is that each of her "backups" involves creative work and keeps her connected to people in the arts. "It helps me to work with people who are interested in what I'm interested in," said Matlock. "It wouldn't be as much fun to me—actually it would feel more like work to me—if I didn't. The best part is that I make my own hours; I find that working for someone else or in part-time jobs becomes intrusive. Even if I became a big star on Broadway, I might still like to take photographs and build Web sites. They're both something I enjoy doing. Though they're side gigs, I think of them as businesses and intend to nurture them and help them grow. I'm investing in upgrading my equipment to professional standards, and I'll take a class or two when I can afford to. I'm a bit hesitant to advertise because I don't want any of these businesses to explode and become my full-time job. Word of mouth seems to be working fairly well for me. But if the time comes when I need to advertise, I will."

Grace Lisle-Hopkins, a photographer, was frustrated after several years of moving from temp job to temp job, only to move on when the inevitable happened—she'd be offered a full-time job. That's great, if you want a full-time job. But for Lisle-Hopkins, thirty-two, jobs were only a means to an end. So she would quit periodically to focus on her art. Finally, she realized that the way to end that cycle was to find a job that followed that rhythm—a job where she could work for a few months straight and then have an expanse of time big enough to get some of her own work done. It turns out that academia was the answer.

As Assistant Dean of Admissions for the School of the Museum of Fine Arts in Boston (where Lisle-Hopkins studied), she works about thirty hours a week, accruing enough hours to take off all of January and then from June through August. The job offers three valuable benefits: (1) expanses of time to work on her art and organize shows; (2) travel to conferences, which affords lots of opportunities to take photographs; and (3) health insurance, the Holy Grail of an artist's life. Another nice piece of the equation is that Lisle-Hopkins works for a Boston institution, earning a Boston-based salary, but she lives in Maine, where the cost of living is significantly lower. For some extra income, she also does administrative work for a library, which also slows down in the summer.

Bonnie Duncan, a teacher/dancer/puppeteer, is married to Dan Milstein, the computer programmer/theater director from chapter 1, and the two of them have talked a lot about what it means to live slash-filled lives. Duncan, thirty, looks at the three different things she does the way a money manager might look at a balanced financial portfolio. Dancing is the high-risk, high-reward activity. It is extremely challenging, but it brings her the most pride and satisfaction of all the work she does. Teaching is the safety net, the work she was educated to do so that she would have a way to support herself. Luckily, she also loves it; but working with young children (whom she teaches to read using drama techniques) would be draining if she did it full-time. As an artist in residence, she works a part-time schedule, splitting her time between various schools that offer the programs she creates. When she needed money (as in before she met her husband, whose higher earnings give her some freedom), she took on more teaching hours. In the future, if she ever needed to support herself, she would add more teaching to the mix.

Dancing and puppetry are artistic expressions that complement each other nicely. Dancing is generally the thing Duncan mentions first and the profession she most identifies with. (She is a dancer with Snappy Dance Theater, a modern dance company that blends theater and dance with acrobatics, puppetry, and martial arts.) Making puppets fuels another part of her artist identity. "I think I wanted to identify myself as my own individual art-making person when I'm not dancing," she explained. "And with puppetry I can do it. Because I can do it in my living room. I can do it by myself. I can do it in small venues. And I don't have to be in tip-top physical shape. If I get injured or if the company falls apart, I'm self-sufficient. And that's what I think I'm figuring out as I get older. That what is important to me, more so than touring the world or being the best, is just making art that satisfies me."

Everything Duncan does is seasonal and cyclical, with busy periods and slower periods. Occasionally, she has to rejigger her schedule, like when she delayed the start of one of her programs with her students so that she could travel for three weeks to take part in a workshop for artists in Florida. "It really wasn't too difficult," she explained. "The schools love having working artists teach the students and they recognize that to do that I need to work on my art."

/ / /

How many times have you said to yourself, "Gee, I'd really like my job if I could only figure out a way to do less of it"? Geoff,* thirty-six and a lawyer/actor-director, seems to have figured that out. I met with him at the offices of Weil, Gotshal & Manges, the law firm he works for in New York City. Aside from the orange messenger bag near the window and his funky sneakers (a suit was hanging on the door, presumably for client or court appearances), he looked the part of a typical lawyer. But unlike the other lawyers at his firm, he has another job. Whenever he's not at the firm, he's working as a theater director.

"I always enjoyed practicing law, particularly engaging in intellectual debates and parsing words and all that kind of stuff, but it was never the center of my pleasures," Geoff told me. He became a lawyer for the same reasons so many people do. In fact, as he told me his story, it reminded me of how I felt about my legal education and the time I spent practicing law— interesting on some levels, intellectually stimulating, but failing to provide a deep sense of fulfillment.

After law school, Geoff spent a few years traveling and then settled in New York. He started devoting time to writing, first short stories and plays and then moving into freelance journal-

---

*He asked that his last name not be used.

ism. Along the way, he got interested in acting and went to acting school, where he discovered he had some talent. That led to directing and eventually a job with the school of the Atlantic Theater, where he directs several student shows a year. All the while he didn't focus on a career path in the law; instead he took temporary legal jobs to help pay the bills, or, more accurately, to allow him to enjoy the trappings of being a corporate lawyer while working as a director. Writing came easily to Geoff and he applied that skill to preparing legal briefs. Having a marketable talent and taking great care in his work distinguished him from other candidates and made him desirable to temp agencies.

One of his placements was with Weil, Gotshal & Manges, who liked Geoff so much, they made him an offer to join the firm as a part-time employee, working by the hour. The work is plentiful, which means he can modify his hours depending on how much he wants to work. And since his work consists completely of writing legal briefs, it's portable. He pointed over to the cell phone, BlackBerry, and laptop on his desk. "With these three things, there's no difference between me sitting anywhere on the entire planet Earth with an Internet connection and sitting here. Most days, I come because it's quiet, they have all the office supplies, and I have a secretary."

What he's traded by working the way he does as a lawyer is a certain amount of career advancement. "I'm not up for partnership consideration, obviously, because that would be absurd," he told me. That's just fine with him, because he wouldn't accept that offer if it were made. His theater work comes first, and though the law is stimulating and has allowed him to buy a house and enjoy other financial goodies, he's got a plan to shift full-time to theater at some point.

Geoff has found a way to practice law that works for him.

SLASH-IN-THE-MAKING /////

Kathryn Squitieri, eighteen, has decided that running an eBay business is the ideal slash for a college student. Squitieri, who goes to Brooklyn College, basically runs a virtual thrift shop, selling trendy clothes in hard-to-find sizes to college girls like herself via her own "eBay store." When I met her at an eBay University seminar, she said was making about $800–900 per month, but the money was only a small part of what she loved about building her eBay business. Squitieri's first part-time job was at a clothing store in the mall near her Brooklyn home where she worked fifteen hours a week for six dollars an hour. In her free time, she was an eBay aficionado, having been online since she was eleven, mostly buying the occasional Barbie doll to add to her collection. Soon she was selling items—her brother's Yu-Gi-Oh! cards, Clinique bonus samples, Chinese slippers, and anything else that was lying around the house. As she explored eBay, she noticed that the kinds of clothing she sold at the mall were circulating around eBay. She started buying clothing on sale and reselling it on eBay and soon learned one of the secrets of retail—buying on the cheap to increase profit margins. That was the end of the job in the mall. "My sister is a size 0 and I'm a 12/14, which means we both have trouble finding clothing," said Squitieri. "So I thought it would be a nice idea to include sizes that are hard to find. I love helping people and making people happy. eBay was never only about making money for me."

Squitieri treasures the autonomy she now enjoys. "It's the best kind of business," she said, "because you are the CEO and you can make your own rules. I can do it at my own time, as much or as little as I want, without a supervisor breathing down my neck. In my school almost everyone works, but I haven't met anyone else who has their own business or is involved in e-commerce at all. They always want to know how my business is doing—whether sales are up around Halloween or Christmas. They've also started to ask if I give lessons."

Like so many ambitious young adults, Squitieri has no idea what she wants to do but says she wants to do everything. She doesn't currently have a major, but is simultaneously studying music, costume design/construction for the stage, geology, and computer information science and e-commerce.

Squitieri is clearly developing a slash mind-set, building her eBay business and learning related skills at the same time as she follows other interests. She says she doesn't have much of a game plan, but she is laying a good foundation. Whether it's through eBay or some other venture, she has already realized that being an entrepreneur is something she enjoys and can do while pursuing other interests.

And one of the main reasons he enjoys being a lawyer is that he isn't doing it full-time. The legal field isn't the only profession where this kind of arrangement could exist. So many professional-sector jobs—from management consultants to bankers and engineers—could support the same setup. If you can imagine negotiating a part-time arrangement to spend more time with your children, why not imagine doing that to make room for some kind of work? Come to think of it, people who go part-time for child-rearing reasons face increased expenses at home, but if you go part-time to pursue a slash, there is actually the promise that your slash will become income-generating even if it's never as lucrative as your primary vocation. (Geoff says he makes about half his law firm salary in the theater.) **The key is to build enough skills and contacts so that if you ever wanted to shrink your working hours, you would be able to negotiate a part-time arrangement with an employer or you could work for yourself as a consultant.** Chapter 8 will give some tips for how to do this.

/ / /

BREAKING INTO EBAY //////

According to the online auction site eBay, more than 724,000 people make a living full- or part-time selling goods on eBay.[1] Today, it's one of the easiest ways to break into business for those with limited capital. It's also attractive because an eBay business can be an almost completely virtual, on-your-own-time kind of sideline. Other than sourcing your inventory and visiting the post office (or a company that handles shipping for eBay stores), you can practically run an eBay business without leaving your home. All of this makes running an eBay business—or other virtual business—an ideal slash.

If that's not enticing enough, the folks at eBay and any number of companies are all clamoring to teach you the ins and outs of opening your eBay business. Training is available in pretty much any medium—from online tutorials and chat rooms to many excellent books, workshops, and even private consultants.

For a quickie education on getting started on eBay, start with the eBay Web site itself, which offers a slew of training options—from chat rooms and discussion boards to online mentors, webinars (Web-based seminars), and subscription newsletters, to name just a few. If you're the type who likes to get a more objective opinion, visit one of the many online communities or blogs serving the eBay seller communities, or buy a book. (Janelle Elms, an eBay selling expert you'll meet in chapter 4, has several titles available on Amazon.com). If you're the type who learns best through live instruction, register for a session at eBay University, the traveling education arm of the company, which holds classes in major cities around the country. One advantage of these live events is that you can mingle with experienced eBay sellers who know all the ins and outs.

One of the only people who asked to use a pseudonym for this book is a woman I'll call Julia Lloyd. She had a high-powered job as a marketing professional while trying to build her own interior design business on the side.

After five months of phone and e-tag, Lloyd, thirty-one, finally e-mailed to say she was ready to get together. I met her through a mutual friend so I thought she was making time for me in her hectic life out of loyalty to our mutual friend. But I realized that part of the reason she wanted to talk to me was that she was trying to make sense of the bifurcated life she was leading. As I questioned her about the various layers of her identity, she was hungry for insights I could share about how other slashes managed to keep it all together.

High energy and bubbly, Lloyd welcomed me into the restaurant she chose for lunch and guided me through her favorite dishes on the menu. She took control even though I was the person who had asked for the meeting. Throughout our lunch, which covered everything from juggling jobs to bicoastal living to dating and children (where and how to fit that in), Lloyd glanced down every few minutes at her Treo, positioned between us on the table. She explained, "The technology is key" in allowing her to meet the responsibilities of her high-powered job while building up her own interior design business. The trickiest part: her clients have no idea she holds a day job and her colleagues are in the dark about her business. She didn't plan for this kind of career.

As part of business school recruiting, Lloyd accepted an entry-level marketing job for a major consumer products company in New York. While most of her classmates were enjoying the relatively carefree life of business school nearing its close, Lloyd was restless to get into the real world even though her job didn't start until the following September. Lloyd had always been interested in design and now that she had some time on her hands, she explored the fields from many angles. She threw herself into working on a television pilot for a reality television show (her idea, "Bachelor Pad Makeover," didn't sell, but Lloyd was onto something; about a year later, *Queer Eye for the Straight Guy* put design reality television on the map). Next, she found herself working on the remodeling of a friend's home, and before long other design projects started flowing in—a room for a prestigious design show; a penthouse apartment. With no formal training but a good deal of artistic flair and savvy, a business was percolating.

Still, she went through with her plan to move to New York and begin the corporate job. "The job allowed me to move to New York City. With my own business, I couldn't even rent an apartment. You need years of tax returns. It's just a tough city to break into as an entrepreneur," she said. The job also provided other benefits—health insurance, a community of other young professionals, and a structure—somewhere to get up and go to every day. "It also let me use the skills I acquired in business school."

At that stage of her business, she spent a lot of time running around to design centers to pick up fabric swatches after hours and during lunch. "Imagine Martha Stewart's early days," she said. "There was a lot of just baking pies." Her plan was to stay at the job long enough to sharpen her skills in the corporate world. She told me she'd know the right time to move on, which would be when her business was big enough to support a staff.

Meantime, the day job she described didn't exactly win points for slash-friendliness. "If they need you for fourteen hours, they have you," she explained. "The pace is so fast—if you miss an hour, the e-mails just pile up." Because she noticed that the company made accommodations for colleagues with small children (and because she doesn't yet have a family of her own), Lloyd justified the rare instances she responded to a client during business hours by treating her business as a "family substitute." Still, she said, she never used company time to handle a client matter without working through lunch or staying late to make up the time. At the close of our lunch, she confessed that she couldn't sustain her current pace indefinitely. "I'm in a transitional phase, a straddle period until I can dedicate myself fully to my business." Before she went back to the office, I asked her what kind of personality a person needs to live her kind of life. "You need to be completely insane, almost like a chameleon, and really driven—knowing why you're doing it—because it's really tiring."

What Lloyd described was working for her, but just barely. When I caught up with her about a year later, her plan had materialized. She had left the corporate job and was now firmly rooted in her own business, though one with many strands. First, there's the straight interior design work for clients. She is also writing a book, working on a pilot for a design-oriented reality television show, and in discussions with a major newspaper about writing a column. "Basically I'm still a slash. But now the slashes are all for me," she said. "I can't imagine doing just one thing."

Lloyd's story, like so many in this chapter, underscores the importance of remaining flexible and knowing when it's time to shake things up. She held on to her corporate job long enough to hone certain skills and bridge a financial gap, but she was willing to adjust as soon as she felt her business was ready. She still approaches her career with a slash mind-set. Whenever I call her to check in, she tells me about a different mix of projects that is pulling her in different directions. The ability to move easily between diverse projects—crucial when she had both a job and a business—is serving her well as she now pursues diverse opportunities all under the banner of her own company.

GETTING TO SLASH / / / /

- Civil servant jobs—with their regular hours and guaranteed income—can be a good way to build security while pursuing a more risky venture.

- Recognize the value of the "virtual, portable, flexible" triumvirate. This strategy leaves lots of room to build a life comprised of multiple slashes.

- Consider the "job plus entrepreneur" model. At the job, you might be able to get training, security, a benefits package, and other perks. In your free-agent life, you'll enjoy autonomy, freedom, and the chance to follow your passions. Together, the two might be the perfect match.

- You can never know when a money gig will turn into a career, but you can stack the odds in your favor by finding a job that you are drawn to for more than its ability to pay the bills.

- Consider commission-based options like real estate and other sales positions. They blend nicely with other work because you can put in more hours when you have the time and your boss generally won't be interested in face-time.

- Sometimes, the ideal slash isn't just one activity, but rather a collection of them.

- Think of your working life as a balanced portfolio. Choose some activities for a guaranteed return on your investment. Choose others that are high-risk/high-return. On a lark, you can even throw in something just because it catches your interest at the moment.

- Take advantage of the rhythms of the seasons—work that follows an academic schedule or is done only in a certain season can provide a guaranteed income for part of the year while leaving long blocks of time available for other pursuits in the "off-season."

- Once you've attained a level of competence in a given field, you're in a better position to negotiate a part-time arrangement with an employer or to work for yourself as a consultant. So it's worth the time to build your expertise.

- Whatever your slash combination, remain flexible and open. What works for you now may not be the right mix in the future, just as what worked for you a few years ago may not be working any longer. ▪

/ **WRITING, TEACHING, SPEAKING, AND CONSULTING: FOUR SLASHES THAT GO WITH ANYTHING**

Just because you love doing something doesn't mean it's wise to do it all day long. I love coaching but the intensity of personal connection also makes it quite draining for me. I find writing extremely fulfilling but, as an extrovert, I need to balance it with human interaction and external stimulation. Workshops, speeches, and interviews are a joy, but after a certain number of hours on stage I have nothing left! I couldn't do any one of these as a solitary endeavor, but when I combine them in the right proportions, each enables the others.

—**Michael Melcher, career coach/writer/speaker**

Lauri Grossman, fifty, has spoken to scores of audiences over the past ten years—from a small group of teachers, to an audience of hundreds of medical professionals at Memorial Sloan-Kettering Hospital and medical conferences around the world. She teaches a semester-long class for doctors and nurses at two schools and has written numerous articles for magazines and trade journals. She is working on a book as well as a number of personal essays, and in the fall of 2005 she was preparing to join the faculty of a new college. She dedicates at least twenty hours a week to these activities. Yet if you ask her what she does, she will say that she's a homeopath, a doctor focused on holistic healing.

"Basically, I was aware of something that could ease people's suffering and could help them feel better in so many different ways. I thought it was just criminal that people didn't know this," she told me. "I was compelled to get the word out, and I would do that using any means possible. If a group of monkeys was having a monkey session, I would have gone to speak to them. It all comes down to the main mission. I'm someone who wants to expose as many people as possible to these ideas, so if I can speak to the doctors and nurses who train others, each of them will then reach hundreds or thousands of others. It's exponential growth."

The speaking, teaching, and writing are all gratifying to Grossman—but they are means to an end. She would do anything to spread the word about homeopathy, so she has identified numerous ways to do that.

In the beginning, she rarely got paid for those lectures, but over time, as her profile grew, a few things changed. First, rather than her knocking on doors asking to be heard, people asked her to speak. Next, an increasing number of those speaking engagements involved a fee.

It helped that public speaking came easily to Grossman, which is why she began with that medium. "I've never had to pick up a book that says how to be a public speaker or a teacher. It's just fun," she said. "If someone told me 'I want you to speak on such and such a topic in front of two thousand people tomorrow morning,' I'd have a restful sleep."

Learning how to be a writer, however, was anything but easy. After 9/11, she was consulted by doctors and nurses to help treat trauma patients. The husband of one of her patients was a writer. "He was so blown away by how well his wife did in the treatment," she said, "that he approached me and asked if I'd be interested in writing a book together."

That book project never got off the ground, but Grossman liked the idea of publishing her ideas, so she decided to work on improving her writing skills. Getting comfortable as a writer required overcoming some longstanding personal demons. "In my freshman seminar at Cornell, a professor singled me out and said, 'I'll do you a favor and tell you never to pick up a pen,' and it took me quite a few years to recover from that," she explained. "But anyone who knows me knows how determined I am. So I went on a quest to find the right teachers. After a few misses, I found an editor who loved me through the process and gave me the confidence to get started." (Full disclosure: after working with that editor for a while, Grossman found her way to me and I then became her private writing instructor.)

Grossman's journey into teaching, speaking, and writing is a common one—the kind that begins when you have a message to tell and you want to take advantage of all the available avenues with which to do so. It's also common for people to find that one medium or another comes more easily. Grossman conquered her fear of writing and found that publishing articles allowed her to reach audiences she'd never have reached had she stuck to her teaching and speaking. She also learned that certain kinds of writing (personal essays and writing about her patients, for example) came easier to her than others (explanatory pieces about medical subjects). Still, she now says she can competently write on most subjects she is asked to write about—a huge leap from where she was when she first heard that jarring comment from her freshman-year professor.

Writing, teaching, speaking, and consulting are four slashes that go with any other kind of work. Think of them as the black pants of a slash wardrobe. Many slash careers have one or more of these activities as part of the mix. The stories that follow explore how different people have given these four modes of expression their own twist and should give you some ideas for how you can add or develop your own skills in these areas.

/ / /

Mary Mazzio, the Olympic rower-turned-lawyer/filmmaker, says she was flooded with requests to speak after she made her first film, *A Hero for Daisy*, a documentary about a revolt by female athletes at Yale University in 1976. "At first, people asked for Chris Ernst, one of the rowers whose story is depicted in the film," she explained. "But Chris is a recluse, so I started to go." Similar to Grossman's experience, Mazzio's public appearances started small—visits to schools to speak with groups of female athletes—and offered little or no pay. But soon she was being booked by larger entities with bigger budgets. In fact, the growth in speaking requests helped Mazzio realize that people were interested enough in her ideas that she had the makings of a film business rather than just one well-received film.

Still, Mazzio does not see speaking as a separate career. "It's really how I promote my films. It's communicating in a non-visual way. If it's not exactly the same, it's very complementary." Mazzio speaks on a range of topics, usually with a connection to women, sports, and the subjects of her films. She controls the quantity of appearances by keeping her fees high. "When you charge a lot, the people who hire you really want you and put a lot of energy into having you there. If you don't charge for what you do, people don't value it."

Writing books could serve the same purpose—delivering her message in another medium—but Mazzio hasn't wanted to commit to a book project, even though requests have been coming in. "I'm dragging my feet because I just can't get excited about it. Writing screenplays [which she did earlier in her career] was so solitary and I really loved it, but I didn't have kids at the time. You have to have an expanse of time to write. If I were exclusively a writer, I'd carve it out. But I don't want to be a triple slash."

Mazzio's experience shows the importance of saying no to adding a slash when it makes sense. Filmmaking is Mazzio's passion, and she is happy to do public speaking now and then in support of that. But she is self-aware enough to know that writing about the subjects of her film, for a medium other than film, would just take her away from making films. **The fact that an opportunity presents itself isn't enough of a reason to take it on. It has to fit in with the rest of what you want to be doing.** *At that moment.*

/ / /

Elizabeth Freedman, thirty-four, stumbled into a career as a public speaker. When she was laid off from a prestigious management consulting job at twenty-nine, Freedman had the first signal that the rosy career she had planned for as an MBA student at Thunderbird in Arizona might not be so easy to achieve. "I was at the company maybe a year. Things were going along beautifully. And then suddenly they weren't," she told me. "I wish I could have seen the writing on the wall. A lot of work. Then less work. Then no work. I survived a couple of rounds, but then it was my turn." The layoff proved financially disastrous for Freedman when her ex-employer went bankrupt before reimbursing expenses. She even had trouble getting her COBRA health insurance benefits. "I began to get seriously pissed off, thinking this is what happens when you put all your eggs in the corporate America basket." Her husband was in graduate school at the time and they relied on her income. At first, she was relaxed, even taking a little trip to Paris, thinking the job search could wait a bit. But when she returned, getting another job was not easy.

In the midst of her search, she and her husband moved from Chicago to Boston, where he got a job. They settled into their new city in July 2001, just before the attacks of 9/11, which further damaged her already disastrous job search. "I just knew that, along with all the other tragedies, there would be the very small but personal tragedy that I wouldn't find work," she explained in her trademark self-deprecating tone. "I continued to network and get job interviews, but the whole process took on a bizarre quality. I had one interview where I was literally offered a job and it was retracted within the same interview. In another, the guy was taking calls from a car dealer selling him a truck. He kept screaming, 'No fuckin' way' into the phone and I'd say, 'This really seems like a bad time. Would you like to reschedule?' Needless to say, no one ever offered me a job. I was fortunate in that I had a spouse with a job, but I did need to work. Oh, and did I mention I gained twenty pounds during this time?"

The weight gain proved fortuitous. Freedman joined Weight Watchers, shed the pounds in five months, and found a community where she felt comfortable. "I always had something to share at the meetings. They called me Chatty Patty. And when it was over, everyone told me I should come and work for the company as a trainer." She thought, "Why not? At the very least, I'd keep the weight off." Around that same time, she also began to work as a personal trainer, teaching spinning classes and weight lifting at a local health club. "Because I had this MBA, I had some pride issues. But I actually loved it all. It was the first time in my life I liked working. I've always struggled with keeping my weight off, so it meant a lot to me to be able to motivate and help people in this way." Still, she continued to go on interviews for "real jobs," convinced that the Weight Watchers and health club gigs were temporary. "But month after month, crazy interview after weird situation, nothing happened. After a while that can get to you. It's a lot of rejection. I was embarrassed; here I am this well-educated person and I cannot get a job. At the same time, I started meeting other people in the same boat. It started to feel like a story."

To lift her spirits Freedman took an acting class at the Cambridge Center for Adult Education. "The class emphasized performing original material and the goal was to come up with a show in which each person performed as an individual as well as in a few ensemble numbers. I felt like I was at summer camp and couldn't have been happier. The teacher suggested I do a mini one-woman show and I chose to make it about my unemployment saga. I called it 'Made Redundant,' because that's what the British called it. It was completely autobiographical. I wrote and wrote and rehearsed and rehearsed, tapping into talents I hadn't used since college. Then, the big night came. My part was only six minutes, but the feedback was really positive. And that was the best feedback I had gotten in over a year."

Based on that feedback, Freedman decided to lengthen her show and work toward performing it before a live audience. Her teacher agreed to help her stage it and she set to work at expanding it to a one-hour show. "The momentum and energy just came from doing something I liked and feeling good about it. Over the next six months I wrote the show in the evenings and on weekends. Around the same time, I became pregnant. And when it was time to do the show, which we did for real in a real theater, I was six months pregnant (great for the parts about gaining all that weight). I wrote a press release, got a few articles in the paper, and the show was sold out for its two-night run. I finally had the glimmer of 'I can do this.'" She wasn't exactly sure what "this" was, but she knew it was something that involved performing in front of an audience. Soon, it became more clear.

The next week, Freedman got her first request for a repeat performance. Based on the local press she received, she got a call from an organization asking if she'd speak in front of a group of 200 unemployed white-collar professionals. She modified the show into a format that worked better for the setting, and it was a hit. Speeches on college and business school campuses followed. Today, she's delivering keynote addresses and doing all sorts of training for young professionals on career issues. (Ironically, a lot of her workshops focus on interview skills.)

It's still a young business so she holds on to the Weight Watchers gig to compensate for dry spells in bookings for speeches. "It's actually a one hundred percent fit for me," said Freedman. "Getting before audiences on a regular basis keeps my skills sharp and I have a lot of flexibility. They send me out to corporate clients where I run their meetings for them. It's exactly what I like to do, talking about something I've experienced. Why we gain and lose weight is something I can literally talk about all day. And weight loss is such a good metaphor for the career stuff. 'You didn't gain it in a day, you won't lose it in a day.' 'You've had a bad day, get back on the horse.' There are even days when I can test out some material I'm going to use in a keynote. I'm a speaker, and if I haven't had a gig in two months I start to miss it. So this keeps me out there, standing up in front of people week after week."

Freedman has built a career out of a bundle of slashes that involves speaking and coaching. Whether she's lecturing to a Weight Watchers group, training a client at the gym, or giving workshops to young professionals, she is using her knack for persuading, teaching, and encouraging people to meet their goals. But, just as other people find balance in pursuing different

SLASH TIP /////

Public speaking is one of the best ways to bring attention to your-self and the work that you do. Yet unless you are perfectly suited to a lifestyle that involves a lot of traveling, speaking as a primary vocation can be exhausting. Trying to work full-time as a speaker can also leave you out of touch with the world you were living in that provided you with fresh content for your speaking gigs. Speaking as a slash solves many of these problems.

Honing Your Speaking Skills

If you're interested in working on your presentation skills, have a look at some of these resources:

- The National Speakers Association (www.nsaspeaker.org). This trade association for public speakers offers a lot of useful information.

- *The Quick & Easy Way to Effective Speaking* by Dale Carnegie (New York: Pocket Books, 1962). This compact classic on the art of public speaking has not gone out of date.

- Toastmasters International (www.toastmasters.org). With chapters in most major cities, this organization offers low-fee membership clubs geared to spiffing up your public speaking skills in a nonthreatening environment.

occupations, Freedman has found balance by using her talent for speaking in different arenas. She has also come up with a combination that provides that desirable mix of a solid foundation (the Weight Watchers meetings and personal training) paired with some activities that are high-risk/high-return (the keynote speeches and career workshops). Most important, she's figured out that she has a versatile gift—something that will serve her well the next time she wants to shake things up.

Freedman is the type of person who comes alive when she gets before an audience. And that is true for so many people who are drawn to public speaking. But even for those who fit that mold, a heavy calendar of speeches can take a toll on the body, especially because professional speaking involves a lot of travel. Freedman has only been in the business for a few years, and is at the point where she is eager for more bookings, so getting burned out is not really a concern for her at the moment.

Freedman says her slash setup has some added benefits in the way she cares for her son. She takes him to a daycare center on the days she meets with clients, gives speeches, or leads her Weight Watchers groups. When she travels and on the weekends, her husband, who works full-time in an office outside the home, is in charge of childcare drop off and pickup. In the end, not getting a full-time office job has left Freedman with a lot more flexibility, a lot more time with her son, and the cost savings of not using day care full-time. It's no surprise then, that many journalists, teachers, consultant-experts, and entrepreneurs do some public speaking when they get the opportunity.

/ / /

Janelle Elms has trained thousands of individuals and companies on how to build or improve an eBay business. It all started with one of those hobbies that evolves first to an obsession, then to a career.

Back in the early 1990s, Elms, now thirty-nine, worked in corporate marketing in a series of fairly uninspiring jobs in Seattle, Washington. In her free time, she discovered eBay, mostly because it was a way to add to her collection of late-nineteenth- and early-twentieth-century valentines with a cowboy theme. By visiting antiques shops, she was able to find the occasional treasure, but once she discovered eBay, the supply seemed endless.

As Elms cruised eBay buying her valentines, she instantly saw a forum where her marketing background could set her apart from other sellers. When she auctioned off a set of collectible patches she thought were worth thirty dollars for over two hundred dollars, she was hooked. During breaks at work and at lunch, she'd run to the computer, posting new items for sale and watching her auctions. In a matter of months, she noticed all kinds of opportunities to build a business on eBay—products she wanted to sell, ways to distinguish herself as a seller, ideas for improving the customer experience. In less than a year, she left her corporate job, replacing it with a series of odd jobs that she juggled for about three years while figuring out how to build a successful business as an eBay seller.

That's when the teaching began. Friends knew she was reveling in her newfound independence as an entrepreneur, and they started asking for advice about breaking into eBay. Elms started running little eBay groups in her home. Around the same time, she attended a lecture at a local university on growing an eBay business. "I knew more than the expert and realized that most of what she was saying was wrong. But until that point, I didn't realize how much I knew," she says. "After the class, I went up to her and asked how she got into teaching. She told me that she was actually thinking of giving it up and asked me if I'd be interested in taking it over. I'd never taught before, never even spoke publicly, but I said yes."

She spent weeks preparing for that first three-hour class, a one-shot lecture the school had given her to test her out. She called it "Don't Throw It Away, Sell It on eBay," and from the minute she stood before the audience, she was lit up by the experience. "I was on a natural high for three days afterwards," she told me. That class was so popular that she was hired to teach another. Then she was hired to teach an advanced class. The classes paid well enough, but Elms was hoping to earn more money, so she decided to put some of her best advice in writing so that she would have something to sell at her lectures. She basically typed up her notes, photocopied them at Kinko's, and month after month sold out every single copy of the home-made book she prepared.

I wasn't surprised to hear any of this because I had seen Elms in action. She was the instructor at a class I took through eBay University, the company's training arm. Elms, in her sensible shoes and sweatshirt, strolled the room where hundreds of established eBay business owners had come to hear her tips for ways to eke more money out of every eBay transaction—how to improve the look of an online storefront; how to avoid payment problems; how to boost international sales. With each revelation, Elms was evangelical about the results business owners could see. And she had data to back it all up. At the end, she was bombarded by audience members rushing to get one of her business cards before she left the room. Along with her eBay advice, she was also sending a message about empowerment through entrepreneurship.

Today Elms lectures around the country for eBay University, does private consulting to the many people who call her after hearing her speak, and writes book after book revealing the secrets to eBay success. Even her volunteer work has an eBay component—she runs three free meetings every month in Seattle for beginners and women's groups. Elms says she enjoys the speaking and teaching much more than the writing, but she makes the time to write books because it's another way to reach people. "There's just so much bad information out there about eBay," she said.

Elms still offers her self-published guides (now packaged as binders so that she can send out updated pages) through eBay and her Web site. In addition, she's published three eBay books for McGraw-Hill, which approached her upon learning about her reputation as an eBay guru. In her free time, she trolls eBay, buying and selling, mostly to make sure that the information she's disseminating is current. "I could never get rid of the

SLASH-IN-THE-MAKING //////

At seventeen, Adam Goldstein, a high school student in suburban New Jersey, has a writing career many adults would envy. It began because he followed an interest: in his case, an obsession with computer programming, particularly on a Mac. He read everything there was to read on the subject and eventually got to meet one of his idols, writer David Pogue, at a book signing. The two talked about nerdy stuff, and a couple months later Pogue contacted Goldstein to see if he'd be willing to be a technical writer on one of his books.

Goldstein, who's now written one book on his own, co-authored another, and worked as an editor on several others for technology publisher O'Reilly Media, says he doubts he'll be a writer full-time. But he knows he'll always write in addition to whatever else he does.

Goldstein writes software, too, which he sells online through GoldfishSoft, a company he founded when he was fifteen. A pretty full plate for a guy who's still in high school, squeezing it all in between his studies, debate team, Quizbowl (a trivia contest), fencing—oh, and being the school president. When I asked his mother how he manages it, her answer: "We're not exactly sure . . . he closes the door and comes out with a book!" What he says: "The more you have to do, the better you are at finding time to do it and the more efficient you become. Of course, I do all these things because I thought they would be fun." And interestingly, Goldstein looks like he's having fun. When I met him at O'Reilly's headquarters in Sebastopol, California, he struck me as a pretty normal and sociable high school kid, albeit one who has taken on some adult-level responsibilities. Because he's turned something he liked to do in his free time into work, he has that ease about himself I saw in so many slashes.

selling," she explained. "If I stopped, there'd be no more books, no teaching, and no consulting. Sometimes I'm so busy that I really miss the selling, the highs of the auction. Then, I'll get right back into it, generating ten to twenty thousand dollars in a month. When I'm touring, it can be as low as a thousand a month. But whatever the amount, I need to stay in it. To keep in touch with the community and my values system."

If Freedman, the Weight Watchers coach/trainer/career speaker, is an example of using speaking skills on a variety of different subjects, Elms has made a career out of the inverse—delivering content on one subject in a variety of formats. Elms shares the eBay expertise she's amassed through private consulting, public lectures, and instructional books. This approach makes sense for anyone who is building a name for themselves as an expert.

Elms's career is also a model of what I call the teaching/ speaking/writing/consulting cycle, in which each slash fuels the others. Once you develop a body of knowledge, it's only natural to deliver that expertise to students, clients, and the public—and to do that means to take on these various labels. Deborah Epstein Henry, the work/life expert first introduced in chapter 2, is another one of those people who has become adept at delivering her expertise in whatever medium is called for. Henry's expert status grew out of Flex-Time Lawyers, the networking and support group she founded in New York and Philadelphia for lawyers balancing their careers with raising a family. Out of that came her consulting practice.

Henry is frequently asked to sit on panel discussions, to deliver keynote speeches, and to author articles on subjects related to her expertise. "It's all been by invitation," she explained. "And once you do a lot of speaking, you're invited to write, and writing is an important way to get the word out to a larger audience. Through the writing, I end up getting more speaking engagements. And when people see me speak, I get more consulting work."

Among experts in any given field, there is a prevailing feeling that at some point you need to write a book to establish your expertise. Henry says she has arrived at that spot. She doesn't have a book yet, but she is feeling the desire to write one. For Henry, it's just a matter of finding the time. "A book is really a wonderful credential," she said. "For me, it's just really a question of when and how I can work it into the repertoire. Often, when you have a book, it's synonymous with the credential. If you don't have a book, you have to have another means to the visibility or platform. If you don't have it, it doesn't mean that you're not an expert, but if you do, it's an obvious way to demonstrate the expertise. It's a wonderful takeaway for people who want to learn from you. I have smaller example of that— like with the articles I write—but I know that a larger example will have even more credibility."

Sally Hogshead, the advertising and branding expert, says she felt this way when she decided to write *Radical Careering*, her first book. The book was critical to relaunching her own career reinvention and to introducing herself to the world in the way she wanted to be seen. For her, being an author is part of a bigger strategy: "The author slash is nestled among others. I had no intent to be author for the sake of being an author. It's a springboard. I'm getting much more involved in being a keynote speaker on a higher level. A book is a calling card for that. Each slash feeds off each other. It's a career ecosystem."

/ / /

In the summer of 2004, Robert Sudaley, the teacher/real estate developer from chapter 3, was ready to write a book. As a middle school teacher who had cultivated a thriving slash career in real estate, he wanted to write a self-help book for teachers and others on a fixed income about how to create wealth through the purchase and sale of real estate. He researched a bit about how nonfiction books were sold and learned that he

WRITING ARTICLES /////

Most of the authors in this chapter got their feet wet by publishing articles on subjects that interested them or about which they had some specialized knowledge. The key to publishing articles is to bring the right idea to the right publication at the right time. With that combination, almost anyone can become a published journalist.

Some Tips on Getting Started

1. Write what you know. It's trite but true: your best shot at getting published as a novice is to write about something you know more about than the average person. When I started writing articles, I used my legal background to find articles that other journalists weren't covering.

2. Start small. If you're just getting started, approach a publication that will work with you even though you don't have prior clips (published articles). Two good places to start: trade publications in your field and alumni publications from any school you attended.

3. Don't expect to be paid at the beginning. Focus on getting experience first, worry about getting paid later.

4. Take a class. Of course you'll pick up skills by taking a good class, but there are other benefits to doing it. Writing can be both frustrating and solitary, so it's essential to start building a network of other new writers. Writing teachers also tend to be good mentors, and all writers need mentors.

Some Useful Resources

- The American Society of Journalists and Authors (www.asja.org). A trade association for freelance writers, this organization offers a lot of online resources, a newsletter, and an annual convention.

- *The Complete Idiot's Guide to Getting Published* by Jennifer Basye Sander and Sheree Bykofsky (New York: Alpha Books, 2003). If you have biases against *Idiot* and *Dummy* books, get rid of them; this one is loaded with great information.

- Mediabistro (www.mediabistro.com). This is an online net-working community for writers. Some of its content requires a membership fee, which is well worth it, particularly the "How to Pitch" series, which gives advice for breaking into various national publications.

- *The Writer's Market*, published annually by Writer's Digest Books (online at www.writersmarket.com). This is a reference guide to thousands of publications and what they look for from writers. The Web site of its parent company, www.writers digest.com, has plenty of resources for new writers, some of which require a membership fee to access.

- *The Portable MFA in Creative Writing*, by the New York Writers Workshop (Writer's Digest Books, 2006). This new book, writ-ten by my colleagues at the New York Writers Workshop, includes an excellent primer on writing magazine articles by one of my first mentors, Charles Salzberg.

would need to find an agent and write a proposal to sell his book to a traditional publisher. In the best of possible worlds, he imagined finishing his proposal, finding an agent, and getting a book contract. He also understood that his book would likely be published at least a year after he began the entire process and that he probably wouldn't be paid a lot of money to write this kind of a guide.

Rather than go through that process, Sudaley decided to publish it himself. He knew he would miss out on the editorial and marketing support a publisher could provide, but he just wanted to get his book out. And he believed that he could do a good job marketing the book to his target audience, other teachers.

Sudaley enlisted the services of Booksurge, a self-publishing company owned by Amazon.com. After four months and an investment of about $2,000 (which included the services of an editor), his book was ready to go. Booksurge prints and ships the books as Sudaley gets orders for them, charging him $5 per copy. He plans to market the book through organizations that cater to teachers.

Sudaley's experience as a first-time author is one way to go. So-called vanity publishing used to be how people who thought of themselves as authors but couldn't convince anyone else of that got their books published. Would-be authors answered ads in the back of literary magazines and bought themselves a bound souvenir copy of their manuscript. In some cases, this still happens. But in many cases, authors are choosing to self-publish and distribute their books instead of trying to work with traditional publishers. Like Sudaley, they do it because they have their own ideas for how to spread the word and sell their books and they want to get a book out quickly.

The vanity publishing industry has undergone a makeover in recent years; in fact, the term "vanity publishing" is rarely used today. Most people (even mainstream publishers) now commonly refer to it as self-publishing. Reputable companies like Booksurge.com, Xlibris, AuthorHouse, and iUniverse have sprouted up in the past few years to help people self-publish. Self-published books rarely make it to the bestseller lists, but there are occasional success stories. In fact, one of the most successful business best-sellers of all time, *Rich Dad, Poor Dad*, was originally self-published by author Robert Kiyosaki.

When Sudaley told me his story, he referenced the self-publishing story of *Rich Dad, Poor Dad*, well-known among readers of business self-help books. Sudaley says he'd be thrilled if a major publisher contacted him after seeing his book, à la *Rich Dad, Poor Dad*'s Kiyosaki, but even if that doesn't happen, he's accomplished his goal of creating a vehicle to share his passion.

THINKING ABOUT A BOOK? /////

If you're considering writing a book, the first question is whether there is an audience for a book on your subject. A good way to get a sense of the publishing market is to start reading some of the industry press. The trade magazine *Publishers Weekly* and the Web site www.publisherslunch.com (a subscription service) can give you a sense of what kinds of books are selling these days.

If you decide that you have a commercially viable idea, you'll have to decide whether to try to find an agent and get a publisher interested or to go the self-publishing route. There are pros and cons to both approaches, as Sudaley's story shows.

The following resources can help you get started.

Books

- *The Guide to Literary Agents*, published annually by Writer's Digest Books.

- *Thinking Like Your Editor* by Susan Rabiner and Alfred Fortunato (New York: W.W. Norton & Co., 2002).

Web Sites

- The Association of Authors' Representatives (www.aar-online.org).

- Mediabistro (www.mediabistro.com). Though it requires a membership fee, the "Pitching an Agent" series is terrific.

BLOG ABOUT IT /////

If self-publishing a book can turn you into an author in a week or a month's time, spreading your ideas via a blog can happen in a matter of minutes. A blog—or weblog—is basically a personal Web site where you can post your musings to the online public. And it's not a one-way experience—anyone can respond to you, and you can choose to publish those responses if you like.

Your blog can be about any subject you choose—from a minute-by-minute commentary on the Mets' current season to a tutorial on Texas Hold 'em or a daily diary of your macrobiotic menus. You serve as writer/editor/publisher, and you're also responsible for making sure other people know about and start visiting your blog. (This often happens when you're discovered by communities, let's say other bloggers, journalists, or Mets' fans, poker players, or macrobiotics who spread the word among like-minded types).

For some people, blogging is a hobby—something they share with a small circle of friends and family, like the holiday season newsletter. But if your blog catches fire and builds a loyal audience of readers, it can increase the reach of your ideas, research, or opinions.

Successful bloggers, like Glenn Reynolds of Instapundit.com, have even snagged jobs with major media outlets (Reynolds now blogs for MSNBC.com). They can also get book deals based on their blogs. (Visit www.stephanieklein.com for a look at an author's blog that resulted in a book deal.)

Blogs might just be the easiest path to publishing. As long as you have access to an Internet connection, it's free to start a blog if you use one of the basic sites like Blogger (www.Blogger.com, owned by Google) or MSN Spaces (www.spaces.msn.com, owned by Microsoft). Blogs are a great way to start putting your ideas out into the world, and also to market yourself and any of your slashes. And if you do get to that book eventually, a blog can be a useful way to promote it.

Some Helpful Resources

Visit www.about.com and go to the page called "Web Logs Basics," which has a nice introduction on blogs. Because the world of blogs is very dynamic, your best bet for current information about blogs is to do a quick Google search on "figuring out blogs"—you'll no doubt turn up countless online posts that demystify the blogosphere.

The preceding examples all show people who figured out a way to teach something connected to their primary vocation. But many people are drawn to teach something that stems from an avocation or passion. Consider the story of Alex von Bidder. He has done both.

Von Bidder, one of the two partners of the world-renowned Four Seasons Restaurant in Manhattan, likes to be identified with several pursuits that barely produce any income—writing, modeling, and yoga. After more than twenty years as a restaurateur, von Bidder, fifty-five, was drawn to yoga practice—as so many people are—to get peace of mind in an increasingly hectic world. As he told me, when I met him in his restaurant one late afternoon between the lunch and dinner rushes, "You don't have to go into a cave and withdraw from activity to find peace of mind, if you know how to access it."

Yoga was so helpful to him that his daily practice became a sacred ritual. And its effects have infused his management style at the Four Seasons, where he says he believes in giving his staff as much freedom as possible and the capacity to make decisions. He also believes that because he is open about his yoga practice and his commitment to meditation, it creates an atmosphere in which others feel that all of their various dimensions are welcome too. So why become a teacher? Why not just engage in a committed yoga practice? Von Bidder said he wasn't really interested in teaching but the studio encouraged him to do it. "I did it for a couple of reasons. One is, I believe, that you really study harder when you teach a subject because then you really have to go deeper. So it helped my practice. And the other is that I'm coming to a stage in my life when teaching what I know has become more important." Von Bidder feels that yoga has changed his life, and he wanted to share that with others.

Von Bidder's comments touch on themes echoed by so many

teachers I talked to—the idea that teaching makes you better at what you teach and that once you're settled into your career, it is fulfilling to share your experience with others. Though people can find joy in teaching when they're young, this struck me as an appealing way to look at the prospect of growing older. People often focus on the challenges of aging, but this attitude puts aging in a new and very positive light.

Von Bidder teaches business as well. He has been an adjunct professor at Cornell University's School of Hotel Administration, and he was also a guest speaker in Professor Srikumar Rao's Creativity and Personal Mastery class at Columbia Business School, which he jokingly refers to as "yoga for MBAs." That class had a huge impact on him and he plans to do it again. As von Bidder put it, "Rao was specifically looking for someone who lives the lessons of yoga in the businessplace, so what I did in my first lecture . . . which was called 'Warrior Wisdom from Yogic Tradition and the U.S. Army,' was meant to elicit the spirit of the ancient disclipine applied to today's life and to dance with it, rather than say 'yes, sir.'" Von Bidder got those MBA students to dance, literally. "Pretty good considering it was a Friday morning 10:00 a.m.-to-noon class and they were all a bit hungover. Classes like that allow me to connect with young and brilliant people, so I really need to stretch, going to the edge of my knowledge and my experience to step through and show them something else. They are so used to business leaders lecturing them on how to make money, but I really believe if you live according to your passions, the money follows automatically."

Von Bidder has also taught a class on manners at New York University School of Continuing and Professional Studies, focusing on general issues and restaurants in particular. "Manners are really about listening to other people, not about what fork to use," he said. "To be gentle in life. To allow other people the space. To avoid surprises. To make things easy. It's all about making it come alive for the class and having fun with it."

Whether he's teaching yoga, creativity in business, management, or manners, von Bidder says it's all the same for him: "It's all about how to live, have fun, and dance with your life."

Because teaching can be done in so many different ways, it fits well with nearly anything else you might do. People teach for so many reasons. Like von Bidder, they teach to pass on knowledge, to give back, and to deepen their own learning. They teach for the extra income. They teach in areas related to their main vocation or in something they consider secondary. They teach because it uses different muscles than the ones they use in other parts of their life. They teach because it just feels good.

Depending on the format they use to pass on knowledge, people who teach take on different titles. They call themselves consultants, lecturers, educators, coaches, tutors. They do it in private workshops, one-on-one sessions, seminar rooms, packed auditoriums, and health clubs. They do it over the Internet and through teleseminars. They do it by writing articles, books, or blogs. They teach what they've studied or what they've learned through life experience. Whatever the reasons and the labels, most teachers find it to be among the most rewarding things they do.

Teaching/Writing: A Tried and True Combination

The teaching/writing coupling is so common that it deserves a mention of its own. Only a tiny portion of doctors teach medical students; but somehow the number of writers who also teach is huge. Why is that? First, writing—even for the most accomplished writers—is often not economically viable on its own. Second, teaching others to write tends to improve one's own writing. Finally, writing can often be a lonely existence; for writers who have a social side, teaching is a natural outlet. I asked two veteran author/teachers—and two of my mentors— why they taught and why so intensely.

Susan Shapiro, forty-four and a memoirist, has been dividing her time between writing and teaching for more than fifteen years. She was one of my first writing teachers and she helped me figure out why the combination is so magical. Shapiro says it's so hard to make a living that you really couldn't come up with a better combination for a writer, especially a fiction writer or poet. "They just work beautifully together. I wake up, do all my writing, and then, with my second energy, I grade papers. I'm going all day alone writing, fighting to put stuff on the computer, and then I go out at night for the human interaction. With the writing, I reach into myself and throw it out there," she said. "When I go out to teach, it's all about getting it back. The smiles. The hugs. The good energy."

All writers complain that teaching takes them away from their writing. But as Charles Salzberg likes to say, "Everything I do takes me away from my writing and I'm always trying to avoid it." A prolific author who teaches about four different classes a semester, Salzberg, fifty-eight, says that around the time of his twentieth book, the thrill of seeing his name in print diminished. "It's old hat to me," he told me. But through his students he gets to experience that thrill again and again. "The best part is when I see someone improve as a writer, even someone who will probably never get published. I get a bigger kick out of a student publishing a book, an article, or an essay than anything I write." Salzberg also finds teaching to be a social outlet. "So much of my social life has to do with people I've met through class. They become friends. It's a sense of a community."

GETTING TO SLASH ///////

- Writing, teaching, speaking, and consulting—the black pants of the slash wardrobe—are four slashes that go with everything. Think of ways you can begin to cultivate one or more of these skills. The tips boxes throughout this chapter will give you some ideas on how to get started.

- Often one mode of expression will come more naturally to a person than the others. If you're a natural speaker, figure out ways to speak more. If writing or teaching comes more easily, create opportunities to pursue that activity.

- The fact that an opportunity presents itself isn't enough of a reason to take it on. It has to fit in with the rest of what you want to be doing. *At that moment.*

- Once you've developed skills as a teacher, writer, or speaker, recognize that you can add slashes by varying the content or venues in which you use those skills.

- Public speaking is one of the best ways to bring attention to yourself and the work that you do; yet speaking as a primary vocation has a lot of drawbacks. Speaking as a slash negates many of those drawbacks.

- If you have an area of expertise, work on all the channels of delivery and take advantage of the teaching/speaking/writing/consulting cycle in which each slash fuels the others.

- Some combinations, like teaching/writing, are common for good reason. Think about trying what has worked for others. ■

CHAPTER 5

ANATOMY OF A SLASH COMBINATION: AN EXERCISE

Some slash combinations coexist better than others. While this isn't a rigid rule, I've noticed a common pattern—the idea of balancing something that isn't very flexible or that requires physical presence with something that is portable, virtual, outsourceable, or able to be done in hourly increments. Remember the old menus in Chinese restaurants that allowed you to pick "one from column A" and "one from column B?" You can do that a bit with your career.

Think of column A activities as the Anchors, those things that require physical presence or are otherwise fixed in some way, and column B activities as the Orbiters, those things that can be done more flexibly. The key is to complement the parts of your life that aren't too flexible with activities that are flexible. If you try to combine too many of the column A Anchors, things can start to fall apart. Adding up a bunch of Orbiters in column B is usually more manageable.

Designating something as an Anchor or an Orbiter doesn't have anything to do with its importance to you or its priority in your life; it just means that the Anchor's logistics are more fixed than the Orbiter's, or that the Orbiter vocation is flexible enough to be done around the constraints of the Anchor.

The beauty is that the moment you think of how to move something from column A to column B, it becomes easier to add something else from column A. For example, if you work as a C.P.A., that job will likely move from column A to column B if you start telecommuting and serving your clients via e-mail and phone rather than reporting to an office each day.

Your Anchors and Orbiters

Try this: List the slashes you want to build your life around. See if there is a natural Anchor for column A, or at least something that at this point in time needs to be your Anchor. It could be the job through which you get your health insurance or steady income, or the place that requires you to show up at an office (or, for that matter, one that requires a lot of travel). Now see if any of your other slashes can go into column B; in other words, whether they can be designed to orbit the activity you put into column A. Typical column B slashes would be writing fiction or building Web sites, work that can be done anywhere and at any time of the day.

List Your Slashes	
Column A: Anchor(s)	**Column B: Orbiter(s)**

If you ended up with too many Anchors, see if you can figure out how to get an activity from column A to column B. You can move any A to the B column by turning it into something you do in a freelance, consulting, virtual, or part-time way—or if you delegate it to someone else. Even caring for your children, the ultimate column A Anchor, can move to column B if your partner stays at home or you have a nanny or other help at home.

The chart below includes some of the slash portfolios that have worked for subjects who were interviewed for this book.

RASHID SILVERA
fifty-nine, high school teacher/fashion model (see p. 129)

Column A—Anchor
Teaching is the anchor; it's what he studied to do and it's his core career.

Column B—Orbiter
Fashion modeling entered his life by chance, and he's pursued that career in a way that works around the constraints of his teaching life.

Why It Works
Teaching is a career with a fixed schedule, a fixed location, and a guaranteed salary and benefits. With school days that end by mid-afternoon, ample vacations, and summers off, Silvera has been able to accelerate his modeling during those periods. Even though he's missed out on some modeling opportunities, he says being unavailable has only made him more desirable to clients. Says Silvera, "It gave them something to figure out—how are we going to get this guy?"

How Long He's Been Doing Both
More than twenty-five years.

NINA FINE*
singer-actor/real estate investor-property manager (see p. 144)

Column A—Anchor
The performing comes first and it's what she considers her professional identity. She needs the freedom to travel for auditions and performances and wanted a money gig that complemented that.

Column B—Orbiter
Fine got into real estate after buying her own home in Philadelphia and seeing the opportunity to buy slightly distressed homes, fix them up, and rent them out. When she inherited a little nest egg, she put it all toward her first investment house. Four years later, she now owns about ten houses. For now, the rent covers expenses with some profit, but she hopes to grow the business substantially by selling the properties as they appreciate in value.

Why It Works
The combination is complementary on many levels. Fine is convinced that the only way to really build wealth is to have your money working for you even when you're not present, which is a principle behind investing in real estate. Performing requires physical presence and is not flexible—when there's an audition, rehearsal, or show, she has to be there. A lot of the work she does in real estate can be done on her own schedule or by someone else.

How Long She's Been Doing Both
About six years.

---

*Actors don't reveal their ages!

GEOFF
thirty-six, lawyer/actor-director (see p. 62)

Column A—Anchor
His work in the theater comes first and is what he thinks of as his career, even though his first educational training was as a lawyer.

Column B—Orbiter
He works about thirty hours a week for a law firm, researching and writing legal briefs.

Why It Works

Geoff has to be present during rehearsals and performances so he needed to find part-time work that didn't require his physical presence. His legal work is completely flexible and portable; he can do it pretty much anywhere on the planet as long as he has Internet access. An added benefit: he's able to work as an artist but with a lot of the comforts of a lawyer's salary. Now that he's established in his legal career, he has started to notice another advantage of working at the law firm—relationships with people who could become patrons of his theater company.

How Long He's Been Doing Both

About nine years.

CAROLYN LANE
thirty-nine, Pilates instructor/art consultant/author (see p. 14)

Column A—Anchor

Her job at the gym is the anchor because it happens in a fixed location, on a fixed schedule.

Column B—Orbiter

All of her entrepreneurial endeavors—art consulting, writing, and private Pilates clients.

Why It Works

For a person with many different professional strands, it's a comfort to have a base job that provides the security of a steady income and benefits. That's Lane's job at the gym. But since that only consumes thirty hours a week (and much of it in the very early morning hours), she has the rest of the day for research/writing at her home office, working with clients (private Pilates clients as well as art clients), visiting galleries, and anything else that comes up. She's an entrepreneur with a cushion.

How Long She's Been Doing Both

About five years.

PART II

SUCCEEDING IN A SLASH LIFE

Part II takes a deeper look at how slash lives work once the pieces are in place—the practical matters like how to present yourself to the world, how to take advantage of synergies, how to overcome obstacles, and how to negotiate work arrangements that allow you to pursue your unique collection of slashes.

CHAPTER 6

**/ PRESENTING YOURSELF:
INTRODUCTIONS, RESUMES,
BUSINESS CARDS, AND MORE**

*Today I have about five different business cards. And I use
different names for the different work that I do.*

> —Ike H., fifty-four,
> psychiatrist/corporate crisis
> consultant

On a balmy September day in 2005, I visited the Great Read, an
outdoor confab of book-related events that was taking place in
Bryant Park, adjacent to the New York Public Library. With
the sun blazing overhead, the speakers on the business journalism panel were casually dressed. One of the men sported jeans
and a baseball cap. Another was wearing a T-shirt with a rock
band's logo on it.

From the start, my attention was drawn to Sally Hogshead, a
striking redhead at the end with a little book perched in front of
her like a funky prop. She looked more like an interior decora-
tor than a business journalist. Then she spoke. Gripping her
tiny book (the only paperback on the panel), she told the story
of how she was an advertising executive who broke into the
world of publishing with an entirely different way of thinking
about books. She briefly mentioned the topic of her book
(strategies for career success), but mostly she talked about its
"look and feel." "More iPod than IBM, more Banana Republic
than Brooks Brothers," she explained.

As Hogshead listed the adjectives to describe her book and the careers it described—sexy, creative, unpredictable, exciting—I thought about how these were the adjectives I'd use to describe her. When the panel ended, she handed out a little accordion-style promotional giveaway for the book—the "mojo cards." Each card had one of her book's "truths" emblazoned on it (e.g., "Jump, and a net will appear"). It was all black and red. Bold and memorable. Just like her.

When I got home, I immediately logged on to the book's Web site and I found more of the same. Fresh and flashy design with an attitude. Sassy and smart interactive insights. Easy to digest. I clicked on the hyperlink to visit her "other life," that of a successful creator of advertising campaigns (the MINI Cooper among them), and the images there had a consistent feel. Hogshead's site conveyed that she was a creative thinker with bold style—whether as a speaker, author, or creator of advertising messages.

Hogshead became an author after an established career in advertising. It was part of a deliberate plan to expand her personal brand and get a particular message out in the world. While she now describes herself as an author, her book is really a vehicle to promote her consulting business and communicate the kind of creative thinking she wants to be associated with. In effect, her book serves the same purpose as a brochure or Web site.

One of the reasons Hogshead's introduction was so effective is that it involved several pieces—her appearance, her book, and her Web site—each of which fills in the picture of who she is and what she is about. That is no accident. Hogshead is an expert in branding and she merely applied an effective branding strategy to her own image.

For Hogshead, disclosing her business background was obviously a benefit in promoting a new identity as an author. She won instant credibility with her audience. But in-person introductions can be tricky for people whose slashes don't have as immediate a correlation as they do for Hogshead.

As you cultivate your various slashes, think about how you want to present your slash identity to others. Many of the slashes I talk to say that the way they introduce themselves, or the parts of themselves they reveal, varies dramatically based on the context. They are adept at leaking out information on an as-needed basis. And often they tell me that having a few possible ways to answer the "What do you do?" question is one of the nifty things about straddling different spheres. Next time you're in a situation with people who don't know you, watch for their reactions when you say various things and think about how it makes you feel to accentuate different parts of your identity.

Mary Mazzio, the lawyer/filmmaker, knows that the minute she tells someone she competed in the Olympics, they have a certain impression of her. "When you're an Olympian, it's like a public validation," she said. "I'm a walking billboard for work ethic and determination. People will sit down and talk to me and sometimes I don't know why. It's just an attractive calling card." And one that has been helpful to her careers in both law and film.

Angela Williams, the lawyer/minister, has had a similar experience. In legal circles, revealing that she's a minister is shorthand for all kinds of associations. "The title of minister just comes with an assumption of integrity and ethics. And you always want to trust your lawyer. For some clients, the whole minister part makes them take a second look—it also makes me memorable, which works to my advantage in many contexts. So much of business success is about how you distinguish yourself from other people, especially when two people come to the table with the same skills."

When I left the law to explore a career in writing, some of the best advice I received came from another lawyer-turned-journalist. "Tell everyone you're a writer," she said emphatically. She then clarified, "I mean everyone you know, everyone you meet, and everyone who asks you what you do. Pretty soon it'll be true."

I was still practicing law at the time. I was also doing some volunteer teaching and studying writing, but I hadn't published anything yet. I felt like a fraud to call myself a writer even though I was spending a lot of time on writing (or, more accurately, figuring out how to write). Still, I listened and noticed that whenever I met new people and said I was a writer, they simply accepted it. They asked me what I was working on and followed up if I saw them again. They also introduced me to other writers, recommended me for writing jobs, and sent story ideas my way. Over time, as I began to incorporate writing more into my life, those words rang truer. Today it rolls off my tongue in a way I never imagined it would, and it's finally true. But saying it helped make it true.

It is equally possible that my foray into writing could have ended differently. I could have explored writing for a bit and decided that it wasn't for me. Or, I could have failed, as I have at other things I've tried. Had either of those things happened, who would have been harmed by my having introduced myself as a writer for a time?

Keith Ferrazzi, the networking maven and author of *Never Eat Alone: And Other Secrets to Success, One Relationship at a Time*, does a variation of this when he "introduces" himself at his workshops. To illustrate the importance of showing your vulnerabilities, he provides the audience with two very different yet entirely truthful statements of who he is. In the first version, he says something like this: "Hi, I'm Keith Ferrazzi, President of Ferrazzi Greenlight Communications. I grew up in Pittsburgh, went to the Kiski Prep School, Yale University, Harvard Business School, became the youngest partner at Deloitte, founded a company with Michael Milken . . ." He then pauses and gives the audience introduction "number two," which begins, "Hi, I'm Keith Ferrazzi, I grew up in Pittsburgh. My father was a steelworker and my mother was a cleaning lady." He says that whether he uses one or the other (or some combination of the two) has everything to do with what impression he wants to make in a given situation.

Many slashes are careful about the right moments for disclosing all the layers of their lives. Oscar Smith, the personal trainer/cop, is open about his dual lives once people know him, but he's not so quick to advertise it to strangers. His training studio's Web site doesn't mention anything about his police work. He prefers that people learn about it once they already have a positive feeling about him. "Some people haven't had a good experience with a cop," he explains. So he'd rather wait and let people get to know him before he gives them a reason to form a preconception.

In 2002, I interviewed Deborah Rivera, an executive recruiter, for an article I was writing about recruiting trends in the financial sector. Two years later, a player at my monthly poker game said he had a slash friend I might want to talk to—Deborah Rivera, an executive recruiter who owns a boutique hotel where she works as a chef on the weekends. I took her number, but it wasn't until I plugged her number into my contact list that I saw her name was already there. When I first interviewed her for the article, I had no idea she had another life. It makes sense that Rivera didn't tell me she was also a hotelier/chef; it didn't have any relevance during our first interview.

On a trip to Seattle to visit my old friend Beth, I met Karen Rispoli, the down-the-street neighbor who drops by with the frequency and dramatic aplomb of *Seinfeld*'s Kramer. My first contact with her was a note she left with a bouquet of hand-cut flowers jammed into the doorway: "Beth's Friend, Welcome to

Seattle!!" Beth had told me that Rispoli was a big presence but she didn't want to give me any of the usual details, like what she did for a living. "You'll get all that when you meet her," Beth told me.

The day after the flowers appeared, Rispoli stopped by unannounced and joined us at the kitchen table while we were finishing up breakfast. Upon hearing that I write about careers, she told me that she was a life coach and had just returned from California, where she had given a presentation on her work. Rispoli uses principles of coaching to work with the families of troubled adolescents—coaching as an alternative to family therapy.

A few nights later, Beth's house was burglarized while we were out for the afternoon. Beth's husband, Peter, came home from work and started looking around, trying to determine how someone could have broken in. "Let's get Rispoli over here," he said to Beth. That's when I learned about Rispoli's second slash—she's a private investigator. And there's another. To complement coaching and private investigating (both of which she does as a free agent), Rispoli, forty-eight, drives a city bus thirty hours a week (the steady job for security and benefits). As we got to know each other, I learned why Rispoli takes time to disclose her various slashes. She said that she's offended when someone asks her "What do you do?" as soon as they meet her. Typically, she'll ask them, "What do you mean by that?" in response. For Rispoli, it comes down to the assumptions people make upon hearing her various job titles. "People look down on you, thumbing their noses at the white-collar/blue-collar thing. It's a tremendous judgment of a person's level of success in life. It's astonishing really."

Having a few identities you can test out on a first meeting is a great way to learn about people's attitudes and prejudices. Other people's assessments of various labels as high or low status was a theme that came up frequently in my conversations with slashes:

> I run into people every day who talk down to me when they think of me as a personal trainer and look up to me when they hear about my other work. It's a great way to learn about people's character.
>
> —Carolyn Lane, Pilates instructor/art consultant/author

> You say you're a real estate broker and it's disdainful. I mean, it was in the *New York Post* the other day on a list of the least-respected professions. And when clients hear I'm a musician, they definitely relax and it's like "ah"; it's a "wow." It's just amazing.
>
> —Ann Guttman, Realtor/musician

> If I'm out meeting new people and say I'm a teacher, the conversation stops. If I say I'm a builder or that I speculate in real estate, people are much more interested and they will listen more.
>
> —Robert Sudaley, teacher/real estate developer

Web Sites: A Slash's Best Friend

Whereas a resume could never convey the multidimensionality of a slash career, Web sites are often perfect for them. After all, slashes are all about hyperlinking to the next thing.

If you visit Michael Melcher's Web site, you'll go on a little journey. Stay within the confines of www.MichaelMelcher.com and you'll learn about his coaching practice, his consulting work, and his educational and professional background in law and business. Click on the "Public Speaking and Media" page and you'll have the option to visit another Web site, Next Step Partners, the folks Melcher teams up with to run his workshops. Curious about the salacious novel he wrote with four Harvard classmates under the pseudonym Jane Harvard? Go to "Overview" (his bio) and click on the hyperlink for *published novel*, where you can read reviews of *The Student Body*, a couple of excerpts from it, and the bios of his co-authors. Interested in his musings about his recent trip to India? Then click on his blog. Showcasing so many aspects of his work/life makes sense for Melcher because clients hire coaches, in part, based on the kinds of professional and life experiences they have amassed.

For Terence Bradford, financial planner by day/hip-hop artist by night, his dual personae are best captured by the photo that greets you when you visit www.bshakes.com, the site of his alter ego Billy Shakes. He's wearing an oversized T-shirt with a do-rag and ball cap on his head, and he's reading the *Financial Times*. His site includes a bio, a statement about his investing philosophy, information on his morning hip-hop market report on Sirius Satellite Radio, and a downloadable song, "Dollar Cost Average." With this one vehicle, he can generate interest in both his music and his financial services business, the two things he is working to connect in people's minds.

Web sites are your public face, the vehicle you use when introducing yourself to clients, consumers, the media, or others who you want to know what you're all about. For certain kinds of careers, they are becoming essential marketing and branding tools—artists, writers, client service professionals, and pretty much anyone with customers can be well served by one.

If you decide a Web site would benefit one or more of your slashes, you'll then need to figure out whether transparency—revealing your various identities in an interconnected way—makes sense for you. The open approach works well for people like Terence Bradford/Billy Shakes who see opportunities for synergy between their different slashes. Obviously it's not the way to go for those who are more selective about sharing their various identities. Some people will have a business card for the day job and a Web site and/or brochure for a creative or entrepreneurial venture. Again, different combinations will dictate different approaches. There is no "one size fits all" slash presentation.

Resumes: Why Have Just One?

Now that laser printing is inexpensive and widely available, the days of visiting the stationer to order your custom-printed resumes are a quaint memory. Today, resumes are fluid. If you're a savvy job hunter, a basic one lives on your hard drive so that you can customize it each time you apply for a job, accentuating those parts of your experience that make you most qualified (and minimizing those that aren't relevant). With a slash career, you can take this concept one step further. Consider adopting the "Geoff" approach.

Geoff has at least three resumes. As a lawyer/actor-director, his various resumes have slightly different formats and purposes. (For a look at Geoff's three resumes and a selection of other resumes and bios mentioned in this chapter, see the Appendix.)

Look at them quickly and you might not even know he's the same person. The "strictly legal" one has his education listed on the top, followed by a section listing all his law-related jobs. There is not a single line mentioning his extensive experience as an actor-director, though in a category called "Other Experience," he lists a series of articles he wrote for newspapers and magazines; as a lawyer, Geoff mostly writes appellate briefs, so anything that shows his writing ability is relevant to a potential legal employer. Even the "Interests" line doesn't mention his theater-related activities.

SLASH TIP /////

A word of caution: if you keep multiple resumes on your computer, be sure to name each file something innocuous, like "Resume Dec07." File names travel with your documents when you send them as e-mail attachments, so if you name your resume "Acting Resume," you might be telling a potential employer who doesn't know you have another work/life more information than is necessary in that context.

Geoff's "actor" resume is in an entirely different format. His name is emblazoned across the top in bolded letters, and beneath that he lists his eye color, weight, and height—information you'd never find on a lawyer's resume, unless the resume was an exhibit in a lawsuit about employment discrimination. The rest of the one-page document is divided into categories—stage, film, television—followed by a section called "Training" and finally "Special Skills." His legal background isn't even revealed in the "Special Skills" section.

He also has a third version, "the director" resume, which emphasizes his theater work but also mentions his legal education. In the event that some day he interviews for a job where an employer could value both his legal and theatrical background, say, as general counsel for a theater company, he would use this one.

/ / /

Bonnie Duncan, the teacher/dancer/puppeteer, has adopted almost the opposite philosophy. She has one resume that presents all aspects of her career. As an artist, performer, and arts educator, all her slashes are interconnected, and she doesn't see any downside to including them all on one resume. She also uses an innovative (though not distracting) approach to font and layout, more evidence that she's a creative person in everything that she does.

In the slash world, there is no limit to the ways people present their skills and background. Mike Franco and Diane Curry, two advertising professionals (and a married couple) who took on a shared slash when they became innkeepers, decided that a joint resume was the best way to present themselves when applying for a position as resident managers of a hotel. They were being hired as a team, so what better way to show a potential employer that they consider themselves a unit, with various strengths and talents between them? This kind of resume also gave them a chance to reveal their personalities, with entries like this in the "Other Skills" section: "Demonstrated ability to talk to a guest and take a reservation while preventing the lemon ginger muffins from burning and still managing to meet the FedEx man at the front door before the second ring!"

That shared resume is just one of several resume-like documents Franco and Curry have to showcase their experience and abilities. They each also have a more traditional resume that documents their respective experience in the advertising field, which comes in handy when pitching a new client for freelance work. Franco also built a Web site, www.clearcutcreative.com, where he posts examples of his creative work. This site is more appropriate than a resume for introducing himself to prospective clients.

The Beauty of Narrative Bios

A narrative bio—a written summary of your background in paragraph rather than bulleted format—is an excellent way of painting a coherent picture of yourself. If you have a Web site, it's likely that you'll post a narrative bio. They are also pretty standard for certain types of careers—writing, speaking, client service businesses, academia—basically any setting where you want to be able to present yourself and your talents to an audience other than an employer. Anyone who deals with customers, clients, investors, or the press would be wise to have a narrative bio. It can be as short as a paragraph or run several paragraphs long; and if you're in the kind of career where they are helpful, you might even want to have ones of varying lengths available for different kinds of requests.

In certain contexts, narrative bios are a signal that you've "arrived." When I asked Mary Mazzio, the former Olympic rower/lawyer who is now an independent filmmaker, for a resume that would help me put things in chronological order, she said, "Gosh, it's been a while since I've had one of those." That's because it's been a while since she's had to apply for a job working for someone else. "At this point, I feel like my work speaks for itself," she added. Most people who are interested in her as a filmmaker and speaker will learn what they need to know about her from the bio posted on her Web site. And she's right—they will also watch her films.

When I was preparing to interview Tim Green, the former NFL player/author/lawyer/television and radio personality, I discovered a couple of narrative bios for him on the Web in a cursory Google search—one for a television show he was anchoring, and one for his law firm's site. The bios are slightly different, but each conveys the many dimensions of his life. He might have submitted a resume to get these jobs, but the narrative bio is what the public sees. It's the place where the various pieces of his life are presented in story format.

Sreenath Sreenivasan, professor and dean of students at Columbia School of Journalism/founder of South Asian Journalists Association/television correspondent, gets so many requests for his bio that he posts several versions of it on his

Web site (www.sree.net)—the "10 second bio," the "in-depth bio," and the "resume version"—so that they are readily available to anyone who might request them. This is a common approach for academics; it's also smart for anyone who expects to be contacted regularly by the media.

What you choose to include in your bio depends on what you want to accentuate and how you want to be perceived by those who are reading it. Deborah Epstein Henry, the expert on helping women lawyers balance work and family, always includes a mention that she is a mother of three in whatever format her bio takes. That fact is as much a credential as any of her degrees or years of experience in the legal community.

Business Cards

When meeting someone for the first time and talking work, it's becoming increasingly common for someone to say, "Take this card. I don't have the card for my other life handy." Then they flip it over and scribble another e-mail, phone number, or the URL for a Web site. **As with resumes and bios, sometimes the best answer for a slash career is to have more than one business card.**

Janelle Elms, the eBay author/consultant/educator, has several different business cards to reflect the various ways she does business. In one incarnation she's an educator/speaker, leading PowerPoint presentations to groups of several hundred at a time about the intricacies of running an eBay business. For those settings, she has a card that directs people to her eBay store, a specialized kind of Web site residing on eBay's site. She does not list a phone number or e-mail address on that site. "I learned the hard way, when some guy called me at 7 a.m. on a Sunday morning with a question, that you can't have a phone number that you give out to hundreds of people," she explained.

For consulting work, she has a more traditional business card, complete with all the ways to contact her. When she goes to estate sales to buy inventory that she sells on eBay, she's learned that prices are better when she uses a card that doesn't have eBay's name and logo emblazoned on it.

Sometimes a slash will inspire a creative idea for a business card. Robert Alper, the rabbi/stand-up comic, uses a card that anticipates a question at the same time that it delivers his marketing message:

Dr. Robert A. Alper
Rabbi/Stand-Up Comic
(Really)

www.bobalper.com

Box 711
East Dorset, VT 05253
1-888-483-3297 (office)
1-802-362-4464 (home)
bob@bobalper.com

Often, a slash will be alluded to in a company name. Joe van Blunk named his film production company Longshore Films in a silent nod to his job as a longshoreman, which he still does when he's not making films. In the same vein, Robert Sudaley, the teacher/real estate developer, used the acronym R.E.A.D. Inc. for his company, Real Estate Acquisitions and Development.

The choice about whether to have one card that conveys multiple slashes or to carry different cards for your various identities is, of course, a case-by-case decision. If you are employed by someone else, you won't have much choice about what your business card says, and you'll likely need another card or cards for your other slashes. For people like me, whose slashes are related and feed nicely into one another, a business card mentioning several slashes doesn't have much of a downside. At the moment, my business card says "Author/Speaker/Coach" under my name. But I get my cards printed cheaply at Kinko's and I tend to tweak those labels periodically as I adjust the activities that comprise my work. Printing up inexpensive cards also makes it easy to have a few different cards, for when you want to keep things separate and when you want to try the all-in-one approach.

One of my longer-term goals is to own a small inn on the beach where I could hold weeklong writing retreats and entertain groups of friends during the summer months. Perhaps in the future, my business card will look like this:

[Side 1]

[Side 2]

Virtual Business Cards, Resumes, and Calling Cards

In cyberspace, people present and spin their identities in all kinds of novel ways. Playing with your e-mail signature is a free and easy way to conduct a mini focus group on your slash presentation and get some free advertising to boot. From the time I knew this book was being published, I added the slash "author" to the list of occupations below my name. After taking on my first few private writing clients, I added the phrase "writing coach" as well. Within weeks of doing that, I got a few inquiries about what kind of coaching I did and whether I was currently available.

The opening page of a blog is another way for slashes to showcase the many layers of their identities. Most blogs have an "about the blogger" page. And in the blogosphere, the more slashes following the name, the more audiences you're likely to attract to your blog. Jonathan Fields, who does quite a lot of things in the area of yoga education and training, used the following labels for himself on his "about me" page when he launched his blog, Unconventional Wisdom: "lifestyle entrepreneur, professional speaker, success coach, author, yoga teacher and lecturer." When I called to ask him about the list, he warned me that there could very well be others added to the list by the time this book is published.

Recently, I've been receiving a lot of requests to post my profile on LinkedIn.com, Friendster.com, and some of the other online networking sites that are sprouting up all over the Internet. These sites are common among people who came of age in the Internet era and are interested in building their social and business networks through the friend-of-a-friend theory of relationships. Here's how it works: you fill out an online form, and within minutes you can post your profile onto a site where thousands of others are doing the same. Your profile lists anything you want to share about yourself—a resume, current work affiliations, organizations you've been involved with in the past, skills that you offer, and so on. Then you e-mail this profile to people you know, inviting them to join the online community you've joined. Once you identify other people you know in the network, you have access to all of their connections within the site.

These sites have become rich resources for employers and recruiters seeking candidates, sales people looking for leads, journalists looking for expert sources—even for people looking to expand their social circles. I posted a profile to LinkedIn so that I'd be able to have a look around, and what I found was a place where the more slashes people had, the more connections they were able to make (and the more likely they were to come up in other people's searches). Have a look for yourself and see if social software sites could be helpful to any/all of your slashes. David Teten and Scott Allen's book *The Virtual Handshake* (New York: AMACOM, 2005) is a good reference on how to navigate this new landscape.

GETTING TO SLASH / / / / /

- As you cultivate your various slashes, think about how you want to present your slash identity to others. Experiment by trying out various introductions.

- Whereas a resume could never convey the multidimensionality of a slash career, Web sites are often perfect for them. Review the examples in the chapter and consider if a Web site makes sense for one or more of your slashes.

- Multiple careers often mean you'll want multiple resumes. Decide whether to have resumes for your different slashes or whether there are instances when an integrated resume makes sense. Always be prepared to start from scratch, creating a custom resume for a particular opportunity; this will be easy to do if you have master resumes from which you can cut and paste.

- If you keep multiple resumes on your computer, be sure to name each file something innocuous because file names travel with your documents when you send them as e-mail attachments.

- Consider whether your career—or any part of it—is better presented through a narrative bio than a traditional resume. Once you create a bio, try to prepare it in different lengths so that you'll have something appropriate for various circumstances.

- What you choose to include in your bio depends on what you want to accentuate and how you want to be perceived by those who are reading it.

- Think about whether a single business card, multiple business cards, or even an innovative combination card is useful for presenting your various slash personae.

- If you're comfortable online, it might be time to expand your network and reinforce your slash identity by using social software tools on the Web. Start exploring. ■

CHAPTER 7

/ SYNERGIES, LEVERAGING,
AND THE POWER OF INCONGRUOUS
COMBINATIONS

Jane Curtin, one of the early cast members of Saturday
Night Live, *sold an apartment at 56 E. 11th Street
this month, according to records filed with the city. The
1900-square-foot three-bedroom co-op was listed for
$1.7 million with Betsy Magee, an independent real
estate broker who doubles as a fitness trainer. Ms. Magee
"is an exclusive personal trainer to CEOs of corporations,
celebrities and groups of runners," according to her Web
site, extremeworkout.com.*

—"Sitcom Star's Co-op Sale," *The
New York Times,* October 30, 2005

It's fairly common to find small squibs about famous people
and their real estate transactions in the *New York Times*. But is it
really relevant to this news item that the "independent real
estate broker" has another job? Probably not, but it's certainly
interesting. And if you were to judge importance based on the
proportion of ink dedicated to Magee, the Realtor/personal
trainer, over the purported subject of the story, Jane Curtin,
you'd think the news was about Magee.

So what does this story show? Simply that people are fasci-
nated by slashes, which is probably why an editor at the *New
York Times* thought millions of readers would want to know that
the real estate broker in this transaction had an unexpected side
gig. Had Magee been a typical real estate agent, she may not

have even been mentioned in the paper and she wouldn't have gotten that free bit of promotion. Garnering interest—whether from the media or the average Jane who hears about your unexpected other life—is one of the nifty little perks of having a slash.

Driving to the beach one afternoon, I was escaping from the traffic by listening to a hysterical report on NPR about sheep suffering from gastric bloat and the methods for treating them. If the story wasn't amusing enough on its own, my ears pricked up when I heard the author credit: "Brought to you by Baxter Black, cowboy/poet . . ." Again, hearing an unexpected combination caught my interest, which is probably the reason the commentator uses that particular moniker.

Whenever I talk to slashes, they invariably tell me about the wonderful things that happen when they reveal an unexpected identity. Sometimes disclosing a slash nets a measurable result like getting a job, attention from the media, a promotion, or a client referral. In other cases, a closer personal connection is made because of the discovery of a shared passion. In still others, it just makes for a richer life. This chapter will highlight some of the synergies and interconnections—planned and unplanned— that result from slash careers and the way people manage them.

/ / /

After a few too many wasted hours in empty apartments waiting for prospective buyers to tour her open houses, Realtor Ann Guttman, who is also a professional musician, realized that these little bits of time would be ideal practice sessions with her French horn. So, she decided to combine her open houses with practice sessions, bringing along her sheet music and stand and playing until people began to arrive. One day, a woman—a broker from a competing agency—walked in and was mesmerized by Guttman's playing. Small talk ensued and the woman encouraged Guttman to come work at her firm, where one of the founders happened to play the classical guitar. They stayed in touch, and about a year later Guttman joined that firm. Once there, she found a community of people who appreciated her not just for her knack for selling apartments, but also for her life outside the firm. "They just adored me, and they never made me think I needed to quit my music career to succeed there," Guttman explained.

During the eighteen years Guttman worked full-time in both fields, music often found its way into her day job. Whereas the French horn open house was a pivotal event, sometimes the intersections were small, warm-glow kinds of moments, like one co-op sale she told me about. Guttman was working on the sale of an apartment for a man whose wife had been a musician but had abandoned a career in music to become a doctor. "It had always upset him that she couldn't make it as a professional musician," said Guttman, who knew about his history since she makes a point of getting to know her clients on a personal level. "So, he was selling his apartment and I got a great offer for him but the board decided not to accept it. He then decided to rent the apartment and—I still tear up whenever I say this—he told me he wanted to rent it to a *musician* at whatever price they feel like paying. It's the most beautiful story ever. I rented the apartment to my best friend and she paid $550 for an apartment that should have rented for $1,200."

Guttman's ability to use her connections to help a fellow musician is part of what has made her real estate career so gratifying. Being a musician is thrilling and exciting, but her position in the business world gives Guttman a way of helping people that she would never have had only as a musician.

/ / /

Joe van Blunk, fifty-one, and a longshoreman/documentary filmmaker, never intended it, but the fact that he's a big burly guy who makes his living working on the waterfront gets him a lot of attention when he starts talking about his arty life as a documentary filmmaker. That he's a Catholic whose first film was about the withering Jewish quarter of South Philadelphia only adds to the effect.

Two days before the film's first screening, the *Philadelphia Inquirer* ran a large story about Van Blunk and his partner Gus Rosanio and their nostalgia for Philadelphia's Jewish quarter. "At the time there was a big gang war in Philadelphia and a lot of the gangsters came from our high school," Van Blunk told me. "The reporter was working on a piece about some guys about our age and then he heard we were making a film. I think he wanted some variety. Maybe he just didn't want to write about gangsters." Defying stereotypes has served Van Blunk well in his artistic pursuits.

Van Blunk has become a regular on the synagogue and Jewish Community Center circuit, where he tells the story of why he made the film to the old timers who usually come up to him and cry after seeing the film. Van Blunk says the idea for the film came to him when he was driving around the neighborhood with his old friend, Gus, now his partner in Longshore Films. "The neighborhood had changed so much since I was a kid and I took Gus there to show him. When we were growing up, it was a very mixed area of Irish, Jews, and Italians, but all blue-collar people. Gus grew up in the Italian section, which was about four or five blocks away from the middle of the Jewish corridor. All he knew was Seventh Street. My section was more mixed."

Van Blunk's father was very friendly with a lot of people in the neighborhood and frequently crossed ethnic boundaries. Said Van Blunk, "Like my father, I was a *shabbos goy*,* so on Sat-

---

*A gentile person who does work on the Sabbath that an observant Jew will not do.

urdays I used to go around and shut off the lights and the stoves in the houses and old synagogues."

"They'd pay me a quarter. I was a Catholic, and this was all so interesting to me. There were these old men and they were talking a different language, but it was just like when I went to church and it was in Latin. These places were just so beautiful with their vaulted ceilings. Later on I came back, riding around, and the writer in me just took it all in. Most of these people had died off and their children moved away, but there were a handful of them left. I pointed out the old synagogues to Gus and the ones I used to go to. A few of them were still active and there were a handful of old Jews in their eighties keeping them alive. As I told Gus, he thought it was an interesting story. From there, it took on a life of its own."

The two returned with a professional photographer, took a series of black and white photographs, and brought them to the *Jewish Exponent*, a local newspaper. Van Blunk wrote some text to accompany the photographs. The *Exponent* published the article on their front page, and Van Blunk was determined to make it into a film.

When the film was shown, the media seized on the story of a self-educated dock worker who had made a sensitive documentary about a vanishing Jewish community. "I certainly didn't design it that way," said Van Blunk. "I just am who I am. I'm from the working class, my family is working class, and it intrigues people that this kind of film was made by someone like me and not an academic. Plus, the idea of a longshoreman is such a heavy stereotype—'the cretin'—and all that imagery of Marlon Brando from *On the Waterfront*. Some people are more savvy and they'll make comparisons to Eric Hoffer, a longshoreman who was a self-taught writer and philosopher who became somewhat of a celebrity in the 1960s. The bottom line is that I work in a closed world even though it exists right in the middle of the city."

Curiosity about his life as a longshoreman has helped spark interest in his films both from the media and from viewers. "After every showing, people are as interested in my background as they are in the film," he says. "People are surprised by their own stereotypes and they expect a filmmaker to come from a certain background, and not one like mine." As long as it means more exposure for his films, that's just fine with him.

In Guttman's and Van Blunk's cases, the synergies between their dual careers were happy accidents. While they didn't intend for one career or identity to help them in another, they recognized when it happened and encouraged it when possible. In other cases, people intentionally create the synergies between their different vocations, highlighting the links for others to see. Terence Bradford is one of those.

Bradford, twenty-eight, is a financial planner by day/hip-hop artist by night, and he fully intends to capitalize on the connections between his two worlds. Bradford grew up in the projects of the Bronx. His mother, single and working two jobs (*not* by choice), lied about their address to get him into better schools. Throughout his education, he traveled among classmates who came from more affluent families. While his college peers from Middlebury College in New York spent summers traveling in Europe, Bradford spent his collecting tolls on the Triboro Bridge and working as a bank teller. After he graduated, he broke into the investment business by using his street smarts and powers of persuasion rather than through the family contacts used by many of his classmates.

All along he was cultivating his alter ego, Billy Shakes, who was gaining a reputation at open mike nights on the hip-hop circuit. Once Bradford got some footing in the financial sector, he realized that his knowledge about money was a way to distinguish himself musically. Now, his raps are peppered with nuggets of financial advice.

His favorite message—that making money involves the same principles, whether you do it illegally on the inner-city streets or legally on Wall Street—is clear in the lyrics to this song:

> *Your coke illegal ever' day of the year.*
> *My Coke I buy legit at $20 a share.*
> *You a gangsta? Then go get your paper.*
> *I'm a paper gangsta getting stock quotes on my pager.*
> *Stocks and drugs both the same in my eyes.*
> *More buyers than the sellers cause the market to rise.*

Bradford/Shakes says he has the same focus whether he's working with investment clients at Primerica or performing his hip-hop act at clubs or college campuses—spreading the word about financial literacy to low-income populations.

Rashid Silvera, a high school teacher/fashion model, has been making connections between two incongruous-sounding careers for more than twenty years. After collecting degrees from Bennington College and Harvard's Divinity School, Silvera landed a teaching job at New York's Scarsdale High School, one of the top secondary schools in the country. By contrast, his entrée into modeling was totally unplanned.

Silvera's career in fashion began when he was in his thirties and was "discovered" on a Long Island beach one summer afternoon. Shortly after that, he got a call from one of the largest modeling agencies in New York to come into the city for a photo shoot. Next thing he knew, he was called up for a meeting at Condé Naste by the president of *GQ* magazine, where he saw images of his face plastered all over the office—on the magazine's cover. When the news of his impending fame hit the high school, Silvera said it took him five seconds to find

SLASH TIP /////

Like many associations, once they are laid out for others to see, they have that of-course-they're-connected kind of quality. So when Bradford becomes Shakes to do the hip-hop morning market report on Sirius Satellite Radio, it's not very surprising. He's a financial guy and he's a rapper, so why not take advantage of any outlet to reach an audience of people who might be interested in his message?

People leading slash lives often see connections between their worlds that are not readily apparent from the outside. Consider some of these:

I have spent years explaining to people on both sides of the intellectual fence that books and football have more in common than most people initially would think. Writing books and playing football require discipline and perseverance. Both require passionate expression of deep-seated emotions. For those who enjoy football and reading books, both are wonderful forms of entertainment and adventurous escapes from a world that is often complex and disturbing.

—Tim Green, former NFL player/author/lawyer/television
and radio personality, from *The Dark Side of the Game*[1]

People think I do these two completely different things— buying art for people and training them in Pilates. But I think of them as very similar. I'm a teacher, coach, or advisor in each, sharing some of my expertise in a way that generally helps people feel better about life. I am a teacher and advisor on two things that are basically luxury services so there is a lot of crossover. A client could come to me in either context or both. I end up teaching Pilates to artists, architects, gallery owners, and other people in the art world. In fact, my gym is my biggest source of art clients. Sometimes, we talk art while doing Pilates and before long the client is asking for advice about buying art. At the same time, when the art clients learn about my Pilates life, they invariably want to try that out. It's a revolving door.

—Carolyn Lane, Pilates instructor/art consultant/author

Psychology is all about developing a way to see the world, helping people to see themselves, seeing what's beneath the surface. It's really what any artist does. In my violin making, I had to train myself to see the wood, the shapes, the scroll, the outline. And the same is true as a psychologist. There, I do lot of work with dreams, which are about images and creativity. The link is really the creativity.

—Robert Childs, psychotherapist/violin maker

Computer programming is this weird invisible art form, but the art is different than in the theater. In the theater the art exists when people see it. It's not what we're doing on the stage but what's happening for the audience. Ideally, in a really well-written computer program, the art is totally invisible to the user. It just makes your life easier and you immediately forget about it. And boy, that's something to be so proud of as a programmer—that you created something so indispensable and easy to use that people will wonder why it was ever done another way. As a programmer, you can solve a problem in a beautiful or very ugly way. But only another programmer may see that beauty. People who aren't programmers can't even understand what you're saying when you say that. Even Bonnie, my wife, who has seen me through some of the problems I've solved, can't really understand. She can be glad that I'm excited.

—Dan Milstein, computer programmer/theater director

out how his new identity would play out with his most important constituents. "The students went nuts," he said. "They just
loved it."

Bearded, dark-skinned, heterosexual, and then thirty-five, Silvera says he was unusual in the fashion industry. He was also
unusual because he worked as a teacher and was up front with
everyone about that from the start. Still, opportunities began
to roll in, with offers to travel to exotic locales for shoots and
daily pay rates from $7,000 to $10,000—about a tenth of the
annual salary he was pulling in from teaching. From the start,
Silvera says he made it clear—both to his modeling clients and
to his school community—that his teaching came first. And he
credits his maturity and commitment to education with ensuring that his head didn't get too swelled. "It's a good thing this
didn't happen when I was twenty-five or else my head would
have been on a swivel," he said. "And what was so beautiful is
that the Scarsdale community immediately realized how my
modeling could be a benefit to the children. Now these kids
were seeing that someone so visible was making the choice to be
a teacher. In the end, it showed them that the children were
worth more to me, not less."

On the modeling front, Silvera says that having somewhere
he had to be every day was probably the best thing that could
have happened, giving him a kind of cachet. "In that world, the
coolest thing you can be is unavailable," he told me. "It just
instantly made me sound so special. So they did everything to
get me. They sent limousines to pick me up, along with someone to give me a massage on the way from school to the city.
And they worked around my schedule, arranging shoots on the
weekends even though that was more expensive."

Silvera acknowledges that modeling afforded him a jet-set
lifestyle he'd never have had as a teacher; it also put him on a

more equal financial footing with the affluent families of his students. Yet when he talks about his slashes, he downplays the financial aspect and instead emphasizes that modeling lets him be a different kind of role model for the students—showing kids a "real life" rather than reinforcing the "those who can't do, teach" aphorism. He relishes sharing bits of his world with them, arranging for internships in the fashion business, and bringing in celebrity friends like Danny Glover to school.

Through modeling, Silvera says he got to feel like a student again, learning as photographers explained to him what they needed from him. "It's just made me so much more empathetic as a teacher," he explained. "I know what it's like when someone takes a picture of you and claims that it's you. But it's just a likeness, a still photograph of a dynamic entity. And I recognized that I was seeing my students in that way. It made me instantly start asking more questions of them. Listening better. Because of my modeling, I learned to give students the time to teach me how they best learned."

As Silvera, now fifty-nine, matured, so did his modeling profile. The glamour remained, but he also secured steady work as the distinguished man with a sly smile and a salt and pepper beard, a regular sight in Land's End catalogs and advertisements for mutual funds, playing a doctor in a white lab coat. Without teaching as the steady anchor, modeling might have been a risky career, especially when you factor in aging. But as a teacher with tenure and a pension, Silvera was able to model when the gigs were available and when he chose.

Silvera turned what could have been a handicap—his unavailability during the school year—into an advantage. And just as his community at school was intrigued by his modeling, so were his celebrity pals impressed by his pride and passion for being an educator. "There is no more important job in the world than teaching children," says Silvera. "If you want to see a celebrity on his best behavior, tell him there's a teacher in his midst. They'll try their hardest to ask an intelligent question. More often than not, it's my teaching that makes me feel like a celebrity."

Synthesis Rather Than Separation

The prior few stories highlight the ways that seemingly incongruous careers are often compatible. Angela Williams, the lawyer/minister, takes that kind of thinking a step further. She says she never thinks of her two professional identities as separate; rather they are parts of a coherent whole. "What you see is what you get, whether I'm in a pulpit, courtroom, or boardroom," she often says.

Shortly after September 11, 2001, when Williams was working as a corporate lawyer at a firm in Washington, D.C., she sent me this e-mail as part of a running conversation we were having about leading a slash life:

> Last week, I experienced what I call "marketplace ministry." At work, I sensed the hurt, pain, grief, shock, and other emotions that my colleagues felt. These emotions affected their productivity. Many were unable to concentrate, made stupid errors, or were reluctant to come to work. Rather than ignoring their emotions, I felt that it was important to deal with it openly in a nonthreatening way. I wanted to validate their feelings of helplessness as individuals as part of the corporate community. President Bush declared Friday, September 14, 2001, the National Day of Prayer and Remembrance for the victims of terrorist attacks. He asked that the people of the United States and places of worship mark this National Day of Prayer and Remembrance with noontime memorial services, the ringing of bells at that hour, and evening candle-

light remembrance vigils. He encouraged employers to permit their workers time off during the lunch hour to attend noontime services to pray for our land.

I felt that people should not have to leave the office in order to attend a memorial service. So that morning, I e-mailed the firm and invited them to join me in prayer in the office's largest conference room. I then prepared a service. At twelve noon, there was standing room only. Practically the entire office showed up—from the mail clerks to the partners. Everyone came together, united by a common denominator—concern for their loved ones and for this country. The emotion was extremely high in the room as people listed the names of relatives and friends who were either dead or missing.

Williams says that incidents like that ad hoc prayer service, where her role as a minister was tapped in the secular workplace, have been common. Likewise, Williams often gets to use her legal skills in her religious community, where she is a leader in various churches and nonprofit organizations. "Churches today are like small corporations," she explained. "A number of them own small businesses, run day care centers, have schools, restaurants, Christian bookstores. They have so much going on that they need to have a corporate mind-set; sometimes they even need to be adversarial. At Christian Service Charities, a nonprofit where I serve as president of the board (and, for a period, interim CEO), I've been able to put into place certain mechanisms you'd normally see on a corporate board—audit, executive, and personnel committees. When we needed to hire a new CEO, I retained a search firm and managed that process, and then trained the new CEO."

Being bivocational, as Williams usually describes herself, even proved to be a benefit to Williams during a six-month period of job transition in her legal career. When she left a position as Deputy General Counsel of Litigation at Sears Holdings Corporation, she was not sure what she wanted to do next. She was working with headhunters and exploring job opportunities, but she also took advantage of the free time to step up her involvement in several community and public service projects. She gave more time to Christian Service Charities; she became associate pastor of a church in an economically disadvantaged community on the south side of Chicago; she served on the Hidden Brain Drain Task Force, a research initiative to foster the advancement of women and minorities in organizations; and she launched a project to create a faith-based community network to meet the needs of prisoners, ex-prisoners, and their families in Chicago. As a person who was technically unemployed, Williams was busier than most people with a full-time job.

Because Williams dedicated herself to her passions, her life "in between" positions did not look very different from her life when she was "working." Not surprisingly, it was through these activities that Williams found her next position, as the Interfaith Liaison of the Bush-Clinton Katrina Fund which is responsible for managing a fund of $20 million allocated to rebuilding churches in communities affected by Hurricane Katrina.

Williams's career looks a bit like that of the politician she might one day become. She follows opportunities and notes that most of the other important positions she has held—as an assistant U.S. Attorney investigating arsons at black churches, on the staff of the Senate Judiciary Committee staff of Senator Edward Kennedy, as a lawyer in a large firm in D.C.—have arisen through an impromptu phone call from someone in her vast network.

Williams gets those kinds of calls often because she makes a point to stay in touch with people from all corners of her life.

Because she's connecting with people about issues close to her heart, those catch-up calls don't feel like networking; they just feel like part of the fabric of her life. Following your passions and sharing your talents are some of the best ways to cultivate a coterie of people who will think of you when appropriate opportunities arise.

Williams's philosophy about work/life ensures that she will never have a gap on her resume. She is always immersed in something meaningful and significant, even during periods when those commitments are for the most part unpaid. **With employers becoming increasingly tolerant of resumes with frequent shifts in position and gaps for childrearing or other personal pursuits, why not recognize the importance of the unpaid activities you do in building skills, experience, and a valuable network?**

Almost everyone who knows Williams is quick to learn that she is both a lawyer and a minister. (She mentions both of her professions in the first sentence of the bio she typically uses for public speaking engagements. See the Appendix for her bio and resume.) This philosophy works for her as her dual careers coexist peacefully; but not all slashes blend so easily, as the next story will show.

When Rivers Converge

John Barr, sixty-two, always knew he was a poet. When he graduated from high school, he announced as much to his parents, who immediately suggested that he go out and get a job. Barr did a lot more than get a job. He went to Harvard College and then on to Harvard Business School and a career in the highest echelons of corporate finance.

The career in banking was the safe thing to do, the path that would ensure he wouldn't "turn into a beach bum," to use his father's words. Barr's life in business was far from anything his father could have imagined. "My dad and all his friends just hated their jobs," he told me. "They lived in a post-depression model where you went to work all day and then went home and did what you loved. I was more fortunate."

All along the way, Barr wrote poetry. And not the kind of rhyming verse numbers read aloud at a colleague's retirement dinner, as was common in the business world. His verses went on for the length of books. Several volumes' worth. Yet in the early days of his career, talking about poetry with his colleagues was another matter. Barr told me that when he started out in the business world in 1972, things were very different. "If my associates at Morgan Stanley were talking about a ball game, I did not feel comfortable talking Yeats," he explained, and then proceeded to give an example. "When I was a brand-new associate/bag carrier, I was traveling with two partners (demigods to me) who knew about my writing and didn't make anything of it. We were traveling to call on the CEO of a large utility company in St. Louis. They were chatting and I was there. This CEO, a lifelong utility man, was complaining about the then-head of the public utility company in his state. He went on to say that the commissioner 'wears an orange jumpsuit to work and is a poet.' What he meant was that he was clearly a kook. The partners looked at me and I was thinking, 'there goes my career.' Just an early example of how the business world viewed poetry. You can see why I didn't bring it up unless other people did."

Barr's poet side and banker side lived separate lives for much of his working life and he referred to them as the "two rivers in my life that have run parallel courses."

In time, Barr started letting his poet side out more and more. As he published books and shared them with colleagues and clients, he received support and positive feedback. Becoming a partner made him more confident, but he says he also noticed an increasing amount of open-mindedness in the business world.

Then, in 2004, Barr's parallel rivers converged when he accepted the post of president of the Poetry Foundation, which had recently received a $100 million gift. By tapping Barr for the job, the nonprofit found itself the ideal leader—an award-winning poet who happened to be a finance professional with more than thirty years of experience as an investment banker, entrepreneur, and advisor to public companies. Talk about a perfect fit. In its press release announcing Barr's appointment, the Foundation quoted him as saying, "The Poetry Foundation is currently known for two things: *Poetry* magazine and the Lily bequest. That combination of literary distinction and financial capability has not occurred before in the history of American poetry. . . . My dream is to see the Foundation built and operated like a well-run company: a company whose business purpose is to provide an important home for American poetry."

Though his own story reveals some challenges, Barr says it shouldn't be surprising to run into a businessman/poet. "In America there is this fascination with the businessman/poet—the archetype being Wallace Stevens—and I can list other people who had full careers in the life of action and affairs," he told me. "T.S. Eliot worked a few years as a bank clerk in London. William Carlos Williams was a pediatrician." In interviews, Barr often mentions William Butler Yeats, one of his favorite poets and one whom many people consider to be the best poet of the twentieth century. Yeats was the founder of the Irish National Theater and he wrote a poem, "The Fascination of What's Difficult," which talks about all the aggravations of putting on a play, staying on budget, and the everyday struggles of an organization.

The merging of twin pursuits, as it happened with Barr, is another common twist on the path of a slash career. Often, a slash is the ideal hire for a job at the intersection of two fields.

Follow Your Passions . . . And See Where They Can Lead

Roger McNamee, forty-nine, is one of those slashes I'd known about for quite some time before getting the chance to meet him. His name turns up from time to time in magazine profiles where he's invariably described as "investment wizard by day/rocker by night." In the summer of 2004, McNamee was in the news again when a spate of those articles announced that he and five partners had founded Elevation Partners, a new firm that would invest in the entertainment industry. The founders also included a genuine rock star partner—someone always mentioned with a slash—musician/activist Bono.

Around that time, McNamee had just written his first book, *The New Normal*, about how best to thrive in an age of much risk and uncertainty when the old safety nets are gone—as are many of the restrictions that lock people into the rat race. McNamee's book shed some light on the ways his involvement in music created some serendipitous connections in his investing career. I traveled to Silicon Valley to learn more about how his two passions affected one another.

In investing circles, McNamee is well-known; in fact, he's something of a "rock star" in that world. In Wikipedia, the online encyclopedia, he's described as "legendary" and "visionary" in the investment and technology industries. In Wikipedia and in many people's minds, however, his music is something he does "in his spare time." McNamee says he does not mind that his music might look like a hobby to an outsider, but as the years have passed, he has come to take it much more seriously. "Music is way too important to me to be merely an appendage to my day job," he told me.

McNamee says he knew the limits of his musical talents from early on. And while he may not have had the gifts to reach the heights of his musical idols, he was good enough to play in several bands. His leadership skills and business acumen helped to make those bands successful. When he was in business school, McNamee played every Tuesday night at a local restaurant. He never missed a performance, even when he had an exam the next day. Throughout his career, he made choices that allowed him to keep music in his life, like marrying someone with a similar passion. His wife, Ann, a university professor/musician, sings in their band, the Flying Other Brothers, so being on the road forty nights a year doesn't mean being away from her. The couple has no children, which frees up a considerable amount of time.

In his early years as a financial analyst at T. Rowe Price, McNamee covered a gamut of industries including aerospace, office supplies, and telecommunications, each of which he studied with great intensity. McNamee can get just as animated talking about paper clips and hole punchers as he can about iPods and music. But once he settled into the technology industry, he found himself in an area where his passion for music was as useful as his knowledge of the industry. His mentor trained him to find an edge that would allow him to know an industry better than anyone else. In technology, McNamee discovered that music, "a little thing that ran through the computer industry," was just the kind of edge that would set him apart.

"I'll never forget when the CEO of one of Silicon Valley's hottest software companies came into my office on his IPO road show," he recalled. "He literally did a double take. He knew me from jam sessions we played in at trade conferences and didn't even realize I was in the investment business. He thought of me as a guy he could relate to from his industry. From my perspective, this was perfect. When you're an investor, CEOs automatically put up their guard because most investors only want to talk about future revenue and earnings. My approach was totally different. I always tried to understand the business issues that mattered to executives. The insights I gathered from these conversations enabled me to add value in a way that was very unusual for a public market investor." Back in the '80s, music was an icebreaker that allowed McNamee to cultivate those relationships.

Over time, success in the investment business gave McNamee both the time and freedom to get more serious about music. The Flying Other Brothers built a following at festivals and clubs throughout the west. They leveraged McNamee's business skills to stage benefit concerts for a variety of worthy causes. The bills for those shows included many of McNamee's favorite musicians and bands. As the Flying Other Brothers got more successful at night, McNamee found ways to bring music into his day job. In 1999, he began a three-year pro bono project for the Grateful Dead, a band that had long been known for its innovative approaches to using technology to stay in touch with its fan base. McNamee volunteered his time to help his favorite band solve a problem in which their music intersected with technology and finance. That experience gave McNamee an education in the music industry and its inefficiencies, and it put him in contact with dozens of other artists, including U2 and Bono. Two years later, Bono called McNamee out of the blue to ask for help on a project to revitalize the music industry. Bono could see that technology was transforming the music business, but he needed an investor's help to do something about it. After several months of business planning,

McNamee and Bono decided to be business partners and launched Elevation Partners.

McNamee's dedication to his music ended up giving him a lot more than an outlet for his creativity; it completely shaped the direction of his career.

/ / /

Many of the people I spoke to said that having multiple vocations makes them better at the various things they do. Through their slashes, they acquired transferable skills and made useful contacts for other parts of their life. Often, a frustration or challenge in one type of work is offset by the complementary nature of an entirely different kind of work. The particular ways that one slash feeds another are as varied as the careers one can imagine combining.

Ann Guttman, the Realtor/musician, says that each of her careers has relieved the stress of the other in some unexpected ways. "As a musician we have all this down time, waiting for the phone to ring," she explained. "It can get you depressed, feeling worthless. I have a lot of energy, so I really needed to fill the space because I was just too depressed when I wasn't working. It really wasn't all about money. The music business is really harsh, so if you were getting hired and then suddenly you're not, it's usually because someone's cousin came to town. It's not really personal. . . . It's a control-of-your-life issue. . . . As a musician you always feel like you have to say yes, so it gave me great emotional freedom to be able to say, 'I don't want to go to Connecticut on the Fourth of July and get stuck in traffic just for five hours of playing an outside job with my music falling all over the place and [being surrounded by] a bunch of drunk people.' Having the other life made me appreciate the times I played much more."

Usually, it's about some variation of that elusive thing we call balance—between stability and excitement, between left-brain and right-brain, between being solitary and being part of a team, between working with one's hands and working with the mind.

Nina Fine, a singer-actor/real estate investor-property manager from Philadelphia, says that her two occupations are complementary on the obvious levels—managing her rental properties provides security when her performing career has dry spells. But her combination also offers some unexpected yin and yang. "Real estate is concrete," she explained. "I know what needs to be done and I do it. And when I do, it's complete. Whereas performing is ambiguous and fleeting; if you missed it, it's over. Plus, when I'm performing, I'm completely surrounded by women and gay men." When she is working on refurbishing houses, she is suddenly in an enclave of maleness, with contractors and handymen. "It's refreshing to be in such a male environment for a change—and it makes me feel powerful as a woman." Fine didn't go into real estate thinking she needed to be around more testosterone, but it is one of the little details of her dual life that she appreciates.

/ / /

Alex von Bidder, whom we met in chapter 4, is well-known among New York City's business elite. Knowing him, a co-owner of the Four Seasons Restaurant, can mean the difference between the equivalent of courtside seats and nose-bleed bleachers in one of the most visible power lunch settings in the world. Von Bidder has had a certain kind of mystique for years, largely based on his proximity to the powerful people who eat at his restaurant. But these days, references to him in the social pages are as likely to be about his yoga instructing, writing, or modeling, some serious slash pursuits that have made him even more intriguing to his patrons and the media.

Followers of New York's bold-faced names have gotten wind of von Bidder's other life, but in the suburbs where he teaches yoga on the weekends, he says many people still have no idea who he is. In fact, if you visit the Web site of Yoga Haven, the studio where he teaches, you'll see a bio that has no reference to his other life. The photo is of a relaxed, smiling man in a fleece sweatshirt, a far cry from the vision of buttoned-up European elegance known to the socialites and executives who see him week-in and week-out at the Four Seasons. His bio is simple and pure yoga: "Alex von Bidder joyously shares what he has learned through yoga: To stand taller, to stretch the mind and to connect with your own brilliance. He attempts to model enjoying the calm at the center of a busy life, especially when that requires inversions of some kind."

Few people take on slashes simply to be more interesting or powerful, and that was certainly not von Bidder's motivation. But sometimes an unexpected professional twist is all it takes to grab a bit of media attention or to distinguish yourself from someone else vying for a job. Sometimes your slash is the thing that someone remembers about you—and therefore a way to deepen a relationship. And sometimes your slash just keeps you at peace—a kind of synergy with yourself.

GETTING TO SLASH / / / / /

- When you (or others) identify synergies among your various slashes, notice the benefits that ensue and think about other ways to capitalize on those synergies.

- If you can see the connections among your slashes, don't hesitate to connect the dots for others. Like many associations, once you lay them out for others to see, they have that of-course-they're-connected kind of quality.

- Examine the ways your slashes can distinguish you from others, give you an edge, or help you build relationships as you cultivate new pursuits. Always work to turn anything that could be a handicap into an advantage.

- Think about whether the training or skills you acquired in one vocation are transferable to another. Often, having multiple vocations can make you better at all of them.

- Get comfortable sharing multiple aspects of yourself in various contexts, when it makes sense to do so.

- Having a slash can be very handy in periods of job transition because it can provide you with a network and activities that might lead to a future position. It can even ensure that your resume doesn't have gaps that are difficult to explain.

- Often a slash is the perfect candidate for a position at the intersection of multiple worlds. Look out for those kinds of opportunities—or create them.

- Often, a frustration or challenge in one type of work is offset by the complementary nature of an entirely different kind of work. ▪

CHAPTER 8 / WORKING THE TWENTY-FIRST-CENTURY WORKPLACE

The quintessential hero of the Forbes *magazine profile doesn't only run an efficient business; he or she plays the flute, paints, explores, performs in a rock band with an ironic middle-aged name like Prostate Pretenders. . . . Mutual fund managers are depicted as cerebral superstars, memorizing baseball statistics, perfecting their piano technique, jetting off to bridge tournaments and philosophy symposia.*

—David Brooks, *Bobos in Paradise*

Picture the offices of a venerated law firm. Oil portraits of the all-male founders hang on the wood-paneled walls in rooms furnished with antiques. Senior partners bring in the work that gets delegated to lesser-ranked partners and associates; associates minister over paralegals, assistants, and librarians, who then, in turn, manage the messengers, technicians, and computers that do the most menial tasks.

Axiom Legal is an entity determined to replace that old-fashioned, hierarchical model with something entirely new. Whether you're looking to hire a lawyer or to work for Axiom, your first encounter with the firm is likely to be through a visit to their Web site, where photos of diverse-looking lawyers have replaced the oil paintings of yore. By eliminating layers of fat (Axiom lawyers work from home or on site at a client and do not have their own assistants), Axiom says it can deliver legal

services more cheaply to its clients while providing a more gratifying work experience for its lawyers. Think of it as a talent
agency for free-agent lawyers. *Cool* free-agent lawyers.

I visited Axiom's office in New York's Soho neighborhood
one steamy summer afternoon as part of my quest to find the
sort of employer that embraces the slash lifestyle. The elevator
to their open floor plan offices was crowded with the architects
and interior designers who inhabit the other floors of this building, across from the hipster haunt Balthazar on bustling Spring
Street. The doors opened into a loft space with hardwood floors
and an egalitarian vibe (no office even for Mark Harris, the
founder and president). Here at corporate headquarters, the
dress code is more bohemian than business casual (when lawyers
meet with clients they follow the client's lead on attire).

At Axiom, white-collar professionals don't have to be bashful
about having other dimensions to their lives. How could they
when the interview includes questions like, "How many hours
would you like to work?" and "Where would you like to work
from?" Lawyers at Axiom not only admit that they want a life
outside the law, they are applauded for it.

Craig Zolan, Axiom's Vice President for Business Development, and Courtney Bowerman, the head of marketing, were
prepared for me. They placed three attorney bios on the table.
"Would you like to meet with the lawyer/filmmaker, the lawyer/
race car driver, or the lawyer who's spending the month of
August in a villa in France while she works remotely for two
Axiom clients?" They also suggested a number of lawyers working part-time while caring for young children. Lawyers tell
Axiom the number of hours they want to work per week and the
length of time they are available to work, and Axiom then tries
to match them with a client project that best fits the lawyer's
availability. Some lawyers work the equivalent of a full-time job
for a while and then take a number of months off to immerse in

another commitment. Others work a regular three-day-a-week schedule for months at a time. There is no standard.

As was the case with so many people I interviewed about their company's flexible policies, Zolan ended the meeting by telling me about a slash period in his own life before he came to work full-time at Axiom. Zolan and his wife founded an online T-shirt company, www.cherrytree.com, while he was working as a contract lawyer for Axiom himself. Since joining Axiom's management, Zolan's wife has taken over most of the responsibilities for the business.

Axiom is but one example of a new-era workplace perfectly suited to the millions of people who seek to work in nontraditional ways. But these companies are not just doing it to please a changing workforce; they're doing it because keeping overhead low makes good business sense.

Resources Global Professionals is an accounting firm that uses a somewhat similar model. Visit their home page, www .resourcesglobal.com, and click on "Becoming Project Professional" to find the following enticing copy:

> Resources Global Professionals is an elite group of individuals who have achieved a new balance between their personal and professional lives. Each of our Associates has at least 10 years of experience in their respective fields, with a proven track record of accomplishment. They're free to work where they want, on a project-by-project basis. All while enjoying the benefits that come with working full time. As a result, they're able to enjoy life on their terms.[1]

For creative professionals, working freelance or as a consultant has long been a reality of working life. But in the virtual age, a copywriter or graphic artist in Iowa can market herself as easily as someone in New York City. The Creative Group, based in Menlo Park, California, caters both to companies

SABBATICALS AND LEAVES OF ABSENCE ////

When I started hearing that sabbaticals and leaves of absence were becoming an increasingly common benefit,[2] my first impulse was to go take a job. As a free agent, it's hard enough to keep the work at bay and stick to a schedule of regular hours, but I also don't get time off to pursue other interests with the assurance that a job will be waiting for me when I return.

First some definitions. A "sabbatical," derived from the Jewish word for the Sabbath day of rest and available mostly in academia, is a period of time taken off from regular work responsibilities. Sabbaticals are customarily taken every seven years and usually with pay. Leaves of absence, which are available across a wider range of professions, refer to any period of time off from work with the permission of an employer. Unlike sabbaticals, leaves are generally taken without pay, but often they allow for the preservation of certain benefits.

If you're itching to explore something new, see if your employer has a policy for people who want to take time off for educational purposes. Policies vary widely about when employees are eligible, how pay and benefits are affected, how much time can be taken, and what employees can do with the time. Whatever the particulars of your employer's program, taking some time off from work without leaving your job is a great way to delve deeper into something and figure out where it's going to fit in with the rest of your life.

At the age when many young professionals are getting settled in their chosen fields, Joel Zighelboim, a thirty-seven-year-old lawyer, took a "time out" to explore other areas that had long been interesting to him. Directly out of law school Zighelboim clerked for a judge, and after that he went to work for Simpson Thacher, a prestigious law firm in Manhattan. He was on the very path to which many young lawyers from elite schools aspire. Financial security was within his reach. To attain it, he knew just what he'd have to do: log grueling hours and continue to be a star performer.

But the promise of a future with that game plan did anything but relax Zighelboim. It showed him that everything was wrong. So after less than a year at the firm, he negotiated a three-month unpaid leave of absence, which he used to take an intensive course in digital filmmaking. The course culminated in a thirty-minute film, a comic documentary he made about bourgeois New York parents' obsession with the newest must-have accessory, the Bugaboo stroller. He set the film to a musical score he wrote himself, and he and his wife aired their pre-parental anxiety as he roamed the city interviewing cliques of parents in different neighborhoods on the stroller choices they had made and what that said about them as parents and consumers.

Once the class was over, it was time to return to the law firm but Zighelboim just couldn't bring himself to go back. Instead, he took a job that ranked lower on prestige but higher on lifestyle, a permanent clerkship for the judge he'd worked for previously. He's been honest with his boss about his goal to transition to film; so honest that he understands he may lose his position one day if she finds someone who's a better long-term fit. But, with evenings and weekends free, he is ready to get to work on his next project and develop contacts. Ironically, his best lead yet in the film world has come from the judge. He is far from settled. With an infant at home, he and his wife (an actress/writer) are now figuring out how being parents fits in among their collective bundle of slashes.

Robert Sudaley, the teacher/real estate investor, juggled his two occupations for about seven years before he decided that he needed to take a leave of absence from school to get his business where he wanted it to be. After nineteen years as a teacher, he was able to stop the clock on his retirement earnings while he spent a year focusing exclusively on his business. After that year off, which was unpaid, he went back to teaching. He will likely quit teaching long before he's eligible to collect retirement at fifty-five, but he'll have access to the financial benefits accrued during all those years as a teacher.

seeking ad hoc creative services and professionals interested in freelance assignments. Sign up on www.creativegroup.com and you can work like a freelancer and enjoy group rates on health insurance; some of their consultants even work full-time, moving from project to project all the while racking up time toward vacation pay and collecting a bonus, without worrying where the next job will come from. Not a bad gig—many of the benefits of an office without the hassle, and *very* slash-friendly. The Creative Group is owned by Robert Half International, the staffing giant that has similar companies for finance, legal, and technology professionals of all levels (see www.rhi.com for descriptions of all of these).

Who'd have thought companies would be vying to offer you ways to work less? While this trend is not entirely sweeping the nation, there are other signs that companies have realized that flexibility can be smart business.

Finding Slash-Friendly Employers

Slashes who want to find a part-time gig would do well to learn from working mothers, who have been the pioneers of workplace flexibility. If flex-time policies, telecommuting, and other alternative work arrangements exist to attract and retain working parents, often they are also available to nonparents who can use the time away from the office for something else that requires large chunks of time.

That's what sculptor Wendy Hirschberg, forty-nine, has been doing for more than twenty-five years, first at Catalyst, which researches and advises on issues around women and work, and then at Ernst & Young's Center for a New Workforce. Both of her corporate jobs involved making the corporate world more flex-time friendly, but she fell into the field entirely by chance. "I was working in a lot of art-related jobs and a friend was worried I was going to starve to death," she explained. "She worked at Catalyst and recommended me for a part-time job. I was interested in feminism so I knew I'd be interested in the subject matter."

After a few years working in what she calls "corporate feminism," the job she took to forestall starvation blossomed into a satisfying career. Hirschberg didn't have children until she was in her early forties, but she had been using her shortened work-week—in the office three days a week and in her studio on the others—to pursue her sculpture long before she added parenting to the mix.

Hirschberg says she has had plenty of struggles along the way—mostly in being taken seriously by both her corporate colleagues and in artistic circles—but she says that honoring her part-time schedule while advancing in her corporate career hasn't been one of them.

Ernst & Young is at the forefront of the flex-time movement, and Hirschberg is convinced that her company's welcoming attitude toward flexible arrangement helps it attract and retain talented professionals. She admits that it's mostly women who take advantage of flexible arrangements, but such arrangements are open to anyone. To reinforce that openness, Hirschberg—who is involved with spreading the word about the company's policies—says her firm has intentionally showcased men, like one who went part-time to become a minister, when talking to the media about their programs.

So how would you go about finding one of these slash-friendly work environments? You can begin by doing some research. **Various entities (including Catalyst, where Hirschberg started out) put out annual "best employer," "best company," or "most family-friendly" lists highlighting companies with the most progressive policies. Each organization judges companies by different criteria, and all of them publish those criteria along with the winners for the year. Generally, the lists will include Web sites for the companies so that you can see where they have offices and**

other details. These are good places to start, even though on the surface some may have a different focus than what you're after.

- Catalyst (www.catalyst.org) gives an annual award "honoring innovative approaches with proven results taken by companies to address the recruitment, development, and advancement of all managerial women, including women of color." Catalyst is focused on women, but companies that have good track records on the advancement of women often have good policies on flexible work schedules, as well as a record of people actually being able to use such schedules without jeopardizing their careers.

- *Fortune* (www.fortune.com) publishes a "100 Best Companies to Work For" list. The magazine tracks a wide range of criteria, much of it having nothing to do with slash-friendly policies, but if you poke around, occasionally you stumble onto useful tidbits like the fact that Starbucks offers health insurance to all employees who work at least twenty hours. *Fortune*'s Web site has archives that go back to 1998.

- Working Mother Media (www.workingmother.com), publisher of *Working Mother* magazine, has been putting out an annual "100 Best Companies" list since 1986. They consider companies large and small, public and private, that complete an application with questions about "all areas of work/life including a company's culture, family-friendly policies and compensation." In a collection of articles, the magazine dices and slices the data in all kinds of ways. As you study the information, be on the lookout for mentions of companies that interpret "flexible" to mean more than "family friendly" (e.g., a company that allows employee time off to train for athletic competitions or pursue artistic talents).

Companies that rate high with the "mature workforce" are also worth a look. These companies recognize the value of a fully trained employee who wants to work fewer hours but does not want to give up work completely. Flexible schedules, job sharing, pension plans, and healthcare for part-time workers are the prime perks in this camp. AARP does an excellent job of tracking these in its annual survey of "Best Employers for Workers Over 50," which is available at www.AARP.org.

Note that variations on these "best employer" monikers have become the must-have accessory among so-called enlightened companies, and that means that the companies on these lists usually post the policies that earned them recognition. That's good news for you—reading through the charts that accompany these surveys or visiting a company's Web site can give you a lot of information formerly only available to someone who has gone through the interview process. After all, "How little can I work and still qualify for health insurance?" isn't generally the best question for a first interview. Every business magazine (*Forbes, Inc., Fast Company*, etc.) has a variation of these lists, and even the ones that are focused more on profitability and growth than working conditions can shed light onto corporate culture. If you're compiling a list of target companies, don't forget that these awards have been going on for years, so check a magazine's archives. Of course, these lists should be a starting point, giving you an idea of companies you might want to research. Remember, written policies are just that; you'll also need to network in your industry and find out what companies are really doing as opposed to what their public relations machines are doing. High performers can often strike deals that are outside the confines of what a written policy seems to provide (similarly, employees who aren't considered valuable will have a much harder time negotiating alternative work arrangements even when a policy exists).

If you're looking at smaller companies, you'll have to do this sussing out on your own. This is where you'll need to listen to word of mouth within your industry and community. While smaller companies may not have comprehensive written policies, they are often able to be more creative because they don't have rigid policies and because they have the freedom not to treat everyone exactly the same.

Sometimes you can learn something about the culture of a small company by the attitude of its leadership. Anne Taintor, who runs the successful greeting card company in New Mexico that bears her name, is a great example of this. Taintor, fifty-three, started her company while she was raising her daughter as a single mother. When I spoke to her, she said that the culture she created for her company grew out of her own experience of needing to have a work situation that recognized the realities of the rest of her life. "Life comes first, and your job comes second," she told me, and the work arrangements of her small staff reflect that. Her business manager usually works four days a week so that she can have time with her horses. One woman takes time off for classes. Another is starting her own business on the side—at least for now it's on the side, said Taintor.

Taintor is very public about these views. Her company's Web site tells the story of her founding the company as a single parent. Though her company has only five employees, she has garnered a good bit of press attention, and nearly every article mentions her background as a single mom. Anyone who goes to such lengths to make her views about work/life known is probably the kind of boss who understands that her employees also have outside commitments.

In Cambridge, Massachusetts, Ignition Ventures, an incubator for science-oriented startup companies, has a similar ring. Ignition operates with only six full-time employees, but it uses a stable of several hundred independent contractors, all with MBAs and Ph.D.s. Founders Amy Salzhauer and Maureen Stancik Boyce both came from rigorous corporate and academic backgrounds, and when they started their company, their mission was to create a business that would allow them and their employees to have lives outside of the office. A visit to the company's Web site is an immediate tip-off to a flex-friendly work environment. On the "About Us" page sits this paragraph:

> *WORK/LIFE BALANCE*
> One of the goals of our company is to provide interesting work for highly qualified managers and researchers. Accordingly, while some of our consultants dedicate all of their professional time to Ignition Ventures projects, others maintain outside interests in academic research, journalism, medicine, investment management, or raising wonderful children.[3]

Salzhauer says that acknowledging the outside-of-the-office lives of everyone involved with Ignition is of paramount importance to her. When an associate in the office was getting married, for example, Salzhauer closed the office for the morning so that all the female employees could join her for a shopping excursion to the Filene's bridal sale. "Of course, if a client needed something, we would have left someone behind," she explained.

Salzhauer, thirty-six, was home on maternity leave with her five-week-old daughter when I interviewed her. While she agreed to talk to me for this book, she said she is prepared to set boundaries between work and home, even as an entrepreneur. (She told me she refused to take a call from an investor while she was in the hospital days after her daughter was born.) "I've given up very lucrative projects because they don't fit in with the values of the firm or the lifestyle we promise to the people who work for us," she explained. "For example, if no one wants to fly to Windsor, Ontario, for a consulting project, we won't take that project even if it made economic sense to do it. We're privately held so we can make those choices."

Among those who work flexibly for Ignition are plenty of working parents, a video artist who splits her time between Ignition and a university, a woman working part-time to care for an ailing mother, and "three people who have been on Zen Buddhist paths," said Salzhauer. "The Zen Buddhists make really great consultants," she added. "Every little detail is important to them."

Of course, Ignition does not hire these folks solely based on their wonderful slash resumes. It hires them because they have the requisite skills to do a particular project. **And using a fleet of highly skilled part-time consultants is a smart business model—it allows the company to assemble the teams it needs on a project-by-project basis without the overhead of a full-time staff.**

/ / /

Whether you're going corporate or working out a deal with a tiny firm, the key to any customized work plan is that your boss be on board. I learned this firsthand when I negotiated a part-time schedule in the legal department of Reader's Digest. I had just moved to Hong Kong and I wanted to work three days a week so that I'd have extra time to travel. It was the first time any lawyer had requested to go part-time in that department; at that time, no one had even modified a schedule to care for a child.

My manager in New York agreed to my request almost immediately. She knew that I was valuable because I was fully trained and enmeshed in the corporate culture. She knew I was also willing to work in a pretty unusual way, making myself available for middle-of-the-night phone calls with clients on occasion because of the twelve-hour time difference. She didn't care what I did with my time off as long as I met my responsibilities to our clients.

But sometimes, moving from full-time to part-time in a context where you've proved yourself can have the opposite effect. When Donna McDonald was transitioning from a career in financial services marketing to her own interior design business, she planned to work part-time in marketing to fund her new business. Initially, she thought the best way to do this was to stay at the company where she had worked for several years. They knew her talents. They respected her. And she had no trouble negotiating a reduced-hours schedule.

When McDonald reduced her hours, however, she found that colleagues kept demanding more of her than she wanted to give. Soon she realized that the only way to make part-time work for her was to go somewhere where she wasn't seen as "McDonald, the Marketing Professional," but rather as an entrepreneur who consulted on the side. She needed a relationship with boundaries.

That's when she was introduced to Sarah Hammann, the chief marketing officer for Posit Science, a San Francisco–based company that develops and markets brain health programs. Hammann was looking to hire a consultant for two days a week and one of her employees recommended McDonald, describing her as an experienced marketer who was consulting on the side while she built her own business as an interior designer. The two met and it was an immediate connection. Hammann, a design aficionado, was intrigued to hear about McDonald's

THE RESEARCH IS ON YOUR SIDE /////

A recent study published in the *Harvard Business Review*[4] encouraged companies to recognize the untapped leadership skills that lie in their minority professionals, a group known for dedicating large amounts of time to their families and communities. If you imagine Harvard Business School as the old guard, then maybe things are changing. According to the report: "Traditionally, to the extent that management takes an interest in employee's extracurricular lives, the focus has been on activities that have long been sanctioned by white male executives and are thought to burnish a company's image or enhance client relationships: United Way drives, symphony orchestra sponsorships, and sporting events, for example." According to the authors of that article, it's high time for a change.

The authors applauded the work of a young manager who gives considerable time to running an award-winning Girl Scout troop in a homeless shelter. Another subject of the study, Demitra Jones, a human resources executive at Pitney Bowes, dedicated thirty hours a month to an African American sorority with a focus on community service. "It's a win-win situation for her and Pitney Bowes and it has been since the beginning. . . . It's no coincidence that Demitra's rapid rise in the company paralleled her progress through the leadership and structure of the sorority . . . ," the authors wrote. This study made the cover of *Time* magazine, so these ideas are sure to be percolating far beyond the Fortune 500 types who read the *Harvard Business Review*.

design work and was impressed with her business skills. There was no confusion about how much of McDonald's time was available, and since Posit Science only needed a certain number of hours, there was also little chance of McDonald being sucked in.

They set up a two-day-a-week schedule with an agreement to swap days if either McDonald's business or Posit Science had a pressing deadline. Because McDonald is able to be open about her design business, she told me she wouldn't be surprised if she got a client referral from someone at the company. A few months after my first interview with McDonald, I e-mailed her to ask if she'd gotten any design clients from her Posit Science relationship. She replied that she'd already landed two—one of them is Hammann.

This negotiation could be lifted from the pages of Cali Williams Yost's book, *Work + Life: Finding the Fit That's Right For You* (New York: Riverhead/Penguin, 2005), a blueprint for figuring out your work/life mix and negotiating with an employer for an arrangement to achieve that. Yost works both with employers and employees as a sort of couples therapist, helping them through the ins and outs of customized work arrangements. Companies hire her to help retain and recruit talent; individuals find her when they're at the end of their rope. Yost recommends committing the deal to writing once it's negotiated, in an agreement that bears some resemblance to a pre-nup.

THE "IF YOU KNEW WHAT THEY KNEW" LIST ////

After reading Yost's book, I asked her to work with me on a top-ten list of things to keep in mind when negotiating a customized work arrangement. Here's what we came up with.

1. If you're good at what you do (and this is a very important piece), an employer will likely choose some of your time rather than none of your time.

2. It's your responsibility (*not* the employer's) to come up with a plan that works for you and for the business.

3. Formal policies are less important than a mutually beneficial arrangement between you and your manager. According to Yost, many large companies have formal policies that are rarely used.

On the flip side, because employers want to keep valuable employees, often you can negotiate a unique arrangement that doesn't fit neatly into the standardized parameters set by the policy writers.

4. If you've already been at your job for some time, it costs a company significantly more to lose you and hire someone else than to come up with a mutually beneficial plan that has you working fewer hours or in a different way. Depending on the type of job you have, experts estimate the cost of turnover as high as 1.5 times your annual salary.

5. Having employees who write plays, spend time with their families, or take sabbaticals is not only good for public relations and recruiting, it can also benefit the bottom line by creating contented employees, enhancing retention, and reducing stress and illness. Make it clear that you're happy to be a poster child for flexibility.

6. If your manager is enlightened enough to consider a flexible schedule, he or she will likely not penalize you for what you want to do with your time (unless, of course, it's something contrary to the company's interests). Your employer's main concern will be how the work is going to get done under your proposed plan and how it will benefit the business.

7. Often employees walk before seeing if it's possible to get a customized work arrangement. What's the worst thing that can happen if you present your proposal? It will be refused. You have nothing to lose, especially if you are willing to leave to find the arrangement you want somewhere else. Chances are, if you're a good employee and you've presented a well-thought-out proposal, your manager will approve some version of your plan for a six-month period. If the answer is no, then your choices are clear—you can stay or you can leave. If you do decide to stay, either for the long haul or as a temporary measure, make sure to diffuse any potential questions about your ongoing commitment by continuing to perform at your previous level.

8. If there is technology that will help you work more effectively, ask for it. You should be prepared to show how the cost of the technology will be offset by some benefit to the company. For example, if you ask for a laptop computer so that you can access

the company's computer network from home, perhaps you can show that you are saving the company money because your assistant is free to work for someone else on the days you are not in the office. Of course, you can also offer to pay for such equipment on your own or contribute to its cost if it's something you need anyway.

9. Believe that it's possible. To succeed in creating, negotiating, and implementing a unique arrangement, you must first believe it's possible. This may require replacing outdated "work happens in the office/during business hours/Monday–Friday" paradigms with the possibilities that exist if you think creatively.

10. Once you've negotiated a customized work arrangement or your manager has agreed to a trial period for your plan, the onus is on you to communicate effectively and to make sure that adjustments are made if you see things falling through the cracks. It's also your job to live up to the agreement and to prove to your employer that that you bring value under the new terms of your employment.

All of this assumes that you are having this conversation with a manager and in a company open to the idea of people working in nontraditional ways. Surely there will be instances when that's not true. Geoff, the lawyer/actor-director from chapter 3, worked as a temp lawyer for several different law firms before settling into his position at Weil, Gotshal & Manges. Once he got there, he worked for a few different partners in the firm before finding those who both valued his brief-writing skills and were comfortable with his being out of the office much of the time. "I wasn't going to be a good fit for someone who wanted to meet frequently with a team for spur-of-the-moment strategy meetings," he told me. For a partner who just wanted well-reasoned and well-researched legal briefs, Geoff was the man.

An increasing number of the most elite and hard-driving work cultures are realizing that even high achievers have passions outside of the workplace. According to a recent *Fortune* magazine article, "As companies learn to accommodate a range of time commitments from top talent, organizations will look less like a pyramid and more like a puzzle."[5] In the world of puzzle workplaces, customized work schedules will no doubt be far more common.

/ / /

After twenty years as a consultant managing complex Enron-type forensic accounting investigations, Karl Hampe, forty-two, realized that he was missing out on too much of life by working ten-to-fourteen-hour days, often through holidays and weekends. The signs were there earlier. At twenty-seven, he was hospitalized for a sudden heart condition after which he vowed to slow down and become more well-rounded. The overachiever in him, however, stepped in and soon he fell into the same patterns, letting work expand to fill all his available time. He was so burned out that he barely had time to look at the book he bought to help him figure out how to find his North Star.

Hampe had an inkling of what he would do with some free time if he could get it—mostly, he wanted to return to his study of cartooning, something he excelled at in college. But before he could even contemplate that, he had to cut the hours he was working. With the same precision he would use on a case, he put together a detailed proposal for the reduced-hours/reduced-salary schedule he sought. His plan covered everything from how to transition workload on existing cases to allocating many of his functions to other personnel so that his skills were put to their highest and best use.

Hampe has a great relationship with his boss, who was supportive of his request from the start; but throughout the negotiation he recognized that his boss had to wear two hats—that of a friend who cared about Hampe's well-being, and that of a manager protecting the company's bottom line. At the same time, Hampe said he had to prove that he was ready to leave if his proposal was not granted, so he put feelers out in the industry and made sure that he had opportunities if he didn't get what he wanted. He made sure his boss knew he was doing this.

His proposal was granted exactly as he presented it, but only after several months of his working full-time while his request made its way through the necessary levels of hierarchy. Hampe's negotiation was successful for several reasons. First, with twenty years of experience, he knew he was valuable enough that his firm would try to keep him. Second, he had tested the waters outside and was willing to leave if his proposal wasn't accepted (both he and his manager knew this, and both pieces are important). And third, he did the necessary work to build the case that the business wouldn't suffer by his altering his schedule. "Companies are realizing that it is in their own enlightened self-interest to keep talented people by accommodating the needs of the whole person," he told me. A junior-level employee with a spotty record of achievement would likely not have been able to accomplish what Hampe did. But at any level, being good at your job is a key ingredient to having this kind of leverage.

When I met with Hampe, he had been on his new schedule for just over a year and was as exuberant as a puppy. He was studying art and cartooning and researching options for syndication and self-publishing. But just as often, he was using his "off" days to sketch at the Metropolitan Museum of Art, sit at cafes, go to the gym, or visit with friends, things that never had a place in his old life. "I just needed some time to recharge and find my equilibrium," he said.

His attitude toward consulting has improved as well. "It feels different because I put less pressure on myself to do everything that everyone could possibly expect of me since it simply is not physically possible in the more limited time," he explained. "I wind up working very hard and managing a lot of delegation, but I feel more relaxed because I know that others believe I am meeting and exceeding their expectations of what a part-time employee can accomplish. Being valued as an individual with a special arrangement is good for my self-esteem and I wind up performing better because of that."

Flexibility Can Happen in Surprising Places.

Any work done in shifts—including medical professionals in hospitals—can be ideal for ramping up or down to accommodate other pursuits. For Sanjay Gupta, the CNN correspondent who was a neurosurgeon before becoming a television correspondent, making room for his CNN job meant taking on half the number of new patients and giving up his research responsibilities at his hospital.

Blue-collar work often has a double advantage—it's done in shifts and it rarely requires you to take it home. Joe van Blunk, the longshoreman/documentary filmmaker, says his work on the docks is especially accommodating to his filmmaking. "I can work ten-hour shifts three days in a row and then take a few days off to be on the set," he explained.

Moonlighting Dos and Don'ts

Whether or not you're out in the open about your various slashes, it's a good idea to think about whether your employer could have a reason to object to any other work that you do. Start by consulting any written employee policies or by checking with the human resources department of your company, requesting confidentiality. If your employer doesn't have an H.R. department, talk with someone you trust in management. These policies may not use the word "moonlighting" specifically; if moonlighting doesn't appear anywhere, look for phrases like "conflicts of interest," "outside employment," or "use of company resources." If you work for a public company, you should also talk to someone in the legal department as you might have to report outside activities to the Securities and Exchange Commission.

When moonlighting policies exist, it's generally because employers are worried that your other work could present conflicts of interests, abuse company resources, or bring notoriety to the company. These policies tend to have common elements:

- They may require notification in writing and permission before you can proceed.

- They may prohibit use of the employer's property for outside employment. (So think twice about using your firm's Mac and color printer to take care of the brochure to market your new line of cosmetics.)

- They may require signing a confidentiality or noncompete agreement, which basically means that you can't use information or intellectual property you obtained from your position for purposes that would be against the interests of your employer (e.g., if your firm prepared a study on hybrid vehicles and you used that study to raise money to finance a company that manufactured hybrid cars, it could be a problem).

GETTING TO SLASH / / / / / /

- Taking some time off from work—as a sabbatical or a leave of absence—without leaving your job is a great way to delve deeper into something and figure out how it's going to fit in with the rest of your life.

- If your employer offers flex-time, telecommuting, or other alternative work arrangements to attract and retain working parents, explore whether these programs are available for other pursuits as well.

- If you're interested in a job with a flexible schedule in a corporate setting, start studying the annual "best employer," "best company," or "most family-friendly" lists put out by various organizations and publications.

- Remember that written policies about flexible schedules are only part of the equation; you'll also need to network in your industry and find out what companies are really doing as opposed to what their public relations machines are doing. High performers can often strike deals that are outside the confines of what a written policy seems to provide (similarly, employees who aren't considered valuable will have a much harder time negotiating alternative work arrangements).

- If you're working or interested in working at a smaller company, listen to word of mouth within your industry and community. Smaller companies may not have written policies, but they are often able to be more creative because they don't have rigid policies and because they have the flexibility not to treat everyone exactly the same.

- Sometimes you can learn something about the culture of a company by the attitude of its leadership.

- Using a fleet of highly skilled part-time consultants is a smart business model—it allows the company to assemble the teams it needs on a project-by-project basis without the overhead of a full-time staff.

- Whether you're going corporate or working out a deal with a tiny firm, the key to any customized work plan is that your boss be on board.

- Being a high performer who brings a lot of value to an organization is probably the best leverage you can bring to a negotiation for an alternative work arrangement.

- Whether or not you're out in the open about your various slashes, think about whether your employer could have a reason to object to any other work that you do. ■

CHAPTER 9

OVERCOMING OVERLOAD, NAYSAYERS, AND OTHER SLASH STUMBLING BLOCKS

If you want to suffer the slings and arrows, be an actor in a rock band. The reaction is constant eye-rolling before anyone hears anything. People just fucking hate the idea of it. But they don't leave the show going, "There's no musical talent there." And it's a hell of a lot of fun.

—Interview with Kevin Bacon, *Breathe Magazine*, September/October 2005

A life pursuing multiple vocations is not without times of stress, overwork, and deep inner questioning. In fact, during my interviews, subjects often asked me whether the periodic doubts or overload they felt were common among slashes. They confessed that at times they didn't have what it takes to be at the top of their game in multiple fields at once. They spoke about instances when one vocation suffered because things were heating up in another part of their life. And a few specifically declined interviews with me because they were just too busy.

Yet even when slashes admit to bouts of hard times, they tend to see such periods as a necessary byproduct of the life they've chosen, not something that makes them question their fundamental choices. When I asked Deborah Rivera what she had given up to pursue the three careers she was managing at the time—executive recruiter/chef/hotelier—she replied, "It required enormous sacrifices. We mortgaged our home and leveraged my business. I wake up every morning with the bizarre combination of being excited and also being scared to death."

Rivera needs to be at the hotel and restaurant every weekend, but because she works with her husband in the business, that is time they spend together; they often blend work with socializing, seeing friends over dinner or a glass of wine at their restaurant. Rivera's weekdays are consumed with her other work as an executive recruiter, but there's plenty of social time in that sphere as well. "My work sends me all over the world," she explained, "and I'm always meeting the most brilliant and interesting people. It's all really fun for me or else I wouldn't be doing it." **That idea—of creating a work/life that suits you so well that it doesn't feel like "work"—is a sentiment many slashes share. It's also why even though they are often putting in long hours, they tend to say that they do not feel overworked.**

After my visit with Oscar Smith, the personal trainer/cop, he invited me to stop in for a workout any time. Clearly, people dropping by to see him at work is a common practice. Smith's schedule—the overnight shift at the precinct, followed by morning training sessions with clients—sounds like it would be exhausting, but it's clear that managing his gym puts him in an atmosphere he'd choose for himself even if he didn't have to be there. He says he has a bit of a reputation for being hard to reach, but if people know him well, they make an appointment or catch him at the studio, where he gets his social fix from chatting with friends and clients. He's also the type of person who manages to return calls within an hour or two, never failing to apologize that it took so long.

Slash careers often involve this kind of blurring of business and professional, work and social. When you take pleasure in your work, something inevitably happens—it stops feeling like work.

/ / /

Getting to that place of comfort usually involves overcoming some hurdles. Whether it's a fear of failure, others' expectations for you, or even your expectations for yourself, most people go through some sort of inner turmoil before developing an unconventional career.

Karl Hampe, the consultant/cartoonist, was starting to feel beaten down after twenty years of intense hours and travel. Though his work was stimulating, he could no longer keep up with the pace of it and was finding himself in a physically dejected-looking posture. "I knew I looked beaten down," he explained. "And I didn't want to be a person who looked like that—the partner stuck in the corner office until 8 p.m., fat, and on his third marriage. It's exactly why our profession is suffering a brain drain. The younger associates think 'there must be more than this,' and then they change firms, but that doesn't solve the more specific issue of finding something that will make them happy."

Hampe began to explore options in other industries. "I tried to find a more 'meaningful' job at a not-for-profit," he said, "but I had some experience in that arena and then my research confirmed that it can be just as much of a grind and I wasn't interested in starting all over from scratch in a field or in proving myself to a new employer."

Hampe says it took falling in love for him to realize that there were other ways to live. When he met his partner, Alan, he got a close-up look at a new way of structuring a working life. Alan is a registered dietician who has built a stable and satisfying career out of a collection of part-time and consulting arrangements. Hampe says he always associated part-time or temp jobs with people who weren't serious or were semi-skilled.

Before meeting Alan, he never realized that highly skilled professionals might end up with a multiple-job approach by choice, not because of a lack of commitment. "Alan gets a benefit in each of his slash jobs from the others and he gets a mix of primary care, private practice, and nonprofit agencies, so he sees clients at different parts of the healthcare continuum," he explained. "It keeps him from getting burned out or jaded and he has control over his hours if he plans far enough in advance. And he's much less dependent on any one employer to make him happy or keep him on the payroll. It seems more like he is in control over his career in his early thirties, when people are usually still working at the mercy of others and hoping to be noticed so they can someday have quality of life."

Hampe says he was envious of Alan at first but gradually came to realize that he could do something similar. When he came to the idea of sticking with his current work but doing it on a flex-time schedule, he said he had a Wizard of Oz moment. "The answer was inside me all the time," he explained. "It was really very liberating, with almost giddy moments. Admittedly it's been a slow transition and the liberating moments were initially less frequent, but they became more and more consistent and the giddiness wore off as soon as I was able to recognize the multicareer/slash option as something that would work for me."

After a process that took more than a year, Hampe has now condensed his consulting work to a manageable three days a week to make room for his creative goals. He is settling into a rhythm for his new life. Because he announced to his firm that he was going to try to become a cartoonist, he gets the occasional "So where are the cartoons?" comment from a colleague, but Hampe knows he is pursuing a creative goal that is pretty elusive, so he has an "instant sense of the inappropriateness" of the question. Choosing a field in which success is such a long shot has also been very freeing, according to Hampe.

Hampe is working on his art, but just as often he is working on things that he would have classified as leisure in his prior life. "Part of what I needed to do was just slow down," he says. Before cutting his hours, he barely had time to think about how people go about making changes in their lives. "I had time to read the snippets available in in-flight or business magazines and a lot of that is superficial. Finally, I was able to read critically, to internalize the thoughts of some smart people, and to decide what was going to work for me." By stepping away from a paradigm in which success was tied to measurable output, he also learned to enjoy the process of self-discovery.

/ / /

Michael Melcher became a career coach/writer/speaker after hitting a serious rough patch in a career that was off to a very impressive start. He earned a combined graduate business and law degree from Stanford University and then traveled to Calcutta and Taipei, where he worked for the Foreign Service. On his return, he joined Davis Polk & Wardwell, a white-shoe law firm. When he left the firm, he worked briefly for a hedge fund and then, after what he called a "timely layoff," launched an Internet startup. It's right out of the early-nineties playbook, including the inevitable crash when his brilliant idea for an Internet company (performing immigration services online) went belly up.

His life hit a low point. Debt. Insecurity. Doubt. "I was treading in quicksand," he told me. It was 2001 and the job market was abysmal. Even if he went back into the field where he had the greatest employability—the law—it wasn't apparent to him that he'd find work easily.

Melcher knew he had the raw material for a career reinvention and started working with a life coach to figure out how to go about doing that. Inspired by how valuable he found the experience of working with that coach, he started toying with the idea of becoming a coach himself. But it wasn't something he could just plunge into. Coaching didn't carry the prestige of his earlier identities and that troubled him. Yet when he announced the idea to his coach, he got the answer he anticipated: "You'd be a fantastic coach!" Next, he had to convince himself that he was okay with the idea. "I had a lot of issues," he told me. "And the funny thing is that the label part was the hardest. With coaching, the label was just not good. It didn't fit with my sense of what I was supposed to be. It had this whistle-on-a-string-around-neck kind of quality, the whole rah-rah thing. I thought it wasn't measurable. And it didn't seem to require all the years of elite education."

Interestingly, Melcher overcame his doubts by using what is basically a self-coaching exercise. He created a written questionnaire that he submitted to about fifteen friends, basically asking them to mirror back to him how they perceived his new plan. The questionnaire included questions like, "Do you think I'd be weirded out calling myself a coach?" and "Do you think I could make enough money coaching?" As he went through this process, he was surprised that a few of the people who knew him best came up with a variation of the same thought, which was that he would grapple with the concept until he began doing it and started getting results and positive feedback from clients. "And that is exactly what happened," said Melcher, who now regularly uses this exercise with his coaching clients. "From the beginning of my coaching work, I knew that the activities were coming to me very naturally and I was having an impact on people. It was something very true for me."

People get there in different ways, but when they hit a point of feeling authentically connected to their life, doubt seems to melt away.

Time Management Techniques for the Overextended

We all have periods when the pressure is on—a deadline is approaching, a show is opening—but for slashes, there are additional challenges. What if the final exam is scheduled for the same day as an important presentation to a client? Or your child's school play falls on the same night as the law firm partners' dinner?

Of course you can't be in two places at once. **But there are a few things you can do to minimize the chances of feeling you need to be. Stay on top of your schedule. Delegate when possible. Build relationships with colleagues who can cover for you in crunch times.** Geoff, the lawyer/actor-director had some interesting thoughts on this subject. "Sometimes you can't tell when a case will blow up for some reason," he said. "When that happens at the same time as I'm busy doing something in the theater, it can be very stressful. I guess there are two ways to deal with it. One is trying to pass the work on to someone else on the case. The other is that I just get really busy. I'll get home at 10 p.m., make a cup of coffee, and work for a few hours. Or I'll get up at 6 a.m. and work till noon on the law and then head right to rehearsal. Luckily, every date in the law world changes. It's scary when they say it's May 3 and you know you have a conflict on June 3 because you realize that things may get put off and it might actually not happen until June 3. So far, I've just been lucky. In six years, I've dodged a few bullets." Like Geoff, many of the slashes I talked to said the dread of conflicts was often worse than the reality.

Geoff's description of just working through the stressful times is something I heard a lot when talking to slashes. "If I can only make it through June, when school break hits," "Until April, when tax season is over," "Until January, when work on the annual report is finished," "Until the summer, when the kids are at camp." Are these pressures really so different from the ones that exist for people with only one career?

While you can't manufacture more time, you can identify techniques to make the best use of the available time you have. Mary Mazzio says the focus techniques she learned as an Olympic rower have been an essential tool for her in balancing the competing demands of being a lawyer/filmmaker/parent. "I used to be an easily distracted person," she said. "I would look up whenever anyone would pass my office at work—always up for a chat." Mazzio says that for quite a while, she was very inconsistent in athletic competitions—either very fast, winning easily, or slow. She went to see a sports psychologist, who had her do some focus exercises, the kind that were being done in the Eastern European countries. For example, she practiced doing math in front of a television with blaring music and people running around. Her focus and concentration improved so dramatically that her racing performance became consistently fast. "Later on, that translated into my work and home life," she said. "It's about committing to something in an unwavering fashion and dedicating your attention to it."

Successful athletes are known for their ability to focus, so it's no surprise that another athlete slash had some good advice about improving focus. In *The Dark Side of the Game*, Tim Green's book about life inside the NFL, he explains how he made use of idle time while sitting in strategy meetings that lasted far longer than it took him to learn what he needed to know:

After battling boredom for several weeks during these long interludes of darkness, I conceived an idea that would enable me to occupy my mind and be free from reproach. I began writing, not with a computer, but by thinking about the material I would put down that night when I was back at home. I would jot notes in the margins of my game plan and on the backs of pages in my playbook, tearing off corners or even entire pages where I had scribbled ideas and scenarios in the weak light of the film projector. My desk at home was constantly piled with scraps of paper that I would consult late into the night while composing newspaper articles, radio commentaries for NPR, or pages and scenes of whatever was my current novel.[1]

Among his many slashes, Green has worked in television, another career with lots of down time. And in perfect slash fashion, he manages to use that down time productively, just like he did when he was playing in the NFL. I interviewed Green while he was getting made up to go on air as the host of *A Current Affair*. During his stint on that show, hired cars took him to and from the airport and studio. During those car rides, and pretty much whenever he has a gap of fifteen minutes, he said the laptop was out. He's written parts of his twelve books this way.

Green is married with four children and told me he rarely works on weekends, which are off-limits for anything other than family time. He'll often decline a barbecue invitation from another family because that would water down the time he spends with his own family. "Basically, I know how to say no and I do it any time something would upset the equilibrium of life," he said. "For example, I live where my kids go to school. This show [*A Current Affair*] was willing to work with me and my needs. But I've said no to a lot of opportunities in television that would have required me to move my family."

Sreenath Sreenivasan, the journalism professor/television reporter/speaker among other slashes, takes this concept to another level. I once saw him respond to his e-mail on a giant screen during a presentation to the staff of the Metropolitan Museum of Art. He does this often, taking advantage of the time while people are trickling into the room where he gives his popular "Smarter Surfing" workshops. He's careful to open e-mails that don't have any private information. And for someone who responds to over a hundred e-mails a day, it's the perfect way to use a scrap of time.

Of course, in some instances, two careers may not actually be compatible, or at least not compatible in the way you've currently configured them. Amy Bloom, fifty-two, the author of several award-winning books of fiction and nonfiction, was a psychotherapist for more than ten years before she began writing fiction. Once her fiction started to take off, she saw the difficulties of running a big practice with patients who required a lot of attention. "The first time I had to do a book tour, it was phenomenally disruptive both to me and to my patients. So I said this kind of practice is just not going to work so well," she said.

Bloom still maintains a small practice, limiting it to patients whose needs she knows well. "It's mostly couples and people I've seen before who need a tune-up. I'd just feel terrible taking someone on and then telling them, 'You're sicker than I thought. You'll need to go elsewhere,'" she explained. "But I just can't be in the emergency room once or twice a month." Bloom also makes sure to confine her patient work to one day a week. "It's hard enough to write, and it would be even harder if patients were scattered throughout the week."

/ / /

Checking in with yourself from time to time to see how things are going is essential for anyone living a slash life. Karl Hampe says his experience using business plans for twenty years at work gave him the idea to do some formal planning as he embarked on his slash life. He sets goals—some very easily achieved, others that will take more work—roughly four times a year, along with the changing of the seasons. Some recent goals include getting a drafting table, finding a low-cost, out-of-the-apartment workspace (he ended up renting a storage locker), and studying how many characters existed in his favorite comic strips. Most important, when he reviews his progress, if he hasn't accomplished A, B, or C, but has done D, E, and F instead, he recognizes his achievements. "One of the easiest ways to get yourself into trouble," he said of his method, "is to set very specific goals, because the world doesn't usually unfold as you expected."

Michael Melcher also does a version of this. He makes a point of periodically doing what he calls "strategic planning for myself." It's the time of year when he looks at the various things that he does—teaching, one-on-one coaching, workshops, speaking, consulting, and writing—and evaluates how everything is going. Sometimes these planning sessions happen when he is alone in his office or apartment, but on occasion, he's turned them into the equivalent of the corporate retreat, booking a week's vacation in Hawaii and bringing along a friend who's game for a joint goal planning session.

Wherever it happens, the process is about reviewing all the activities he's currently doing, assessing the purpose for each, and figuring out what stays, what goes, and what gets tweaked. "With any business, you have to constantly prune to see where growth occurred," he said. Inevitably, he learns something surprising. One year, he counted all the coaching appointments he did in the course of a year and analyzed the distribution of how many people he saw on a given day. In the end, he realized that he could do the same number of appointments during only two days a week, restricting his appointments for coaching to Tuesdays and Thursdays. "You really have to look at the data. One of the fascinating things I learned is that about seventy to eighty days a year I had just one appointment, yet I perceived myself as completely booked all the time."

That revelation was crucial in his becoming more productive. "The different things I do require different kinds of energy," he explained. "On my writing days, I'm internally directed and I don't want to be responsible to other people. I may be at home or in the office. I might be casual or dressed up. But I limit all external things. I don't have lunch. I don't check e-mail. I avoid phone calls. Coaching needs a different kind of energy. And when I was switching from one to the other in the same day, I just wasn't as effective. There were days when I felt resentful with a client coming in because I was rushing to get something done. That is not good if you're a coach. Once I created this structure, it was a relief to just focus on clients those two days. Even administrative work has its own energy and needs its own space."

For Dan Milstein, the computer programmer/theater director, the answer to time management was coming up with a tentative daily schedule. Milstein has a life where a good chunk of the work he needs to do each day—programming for his clients and troubleshooting for his theater company—can be done at home. But home is loaded with distractions—the dog, the pile of bills screaming to be sorted, every last section of the newspaper, the laundry. The bulk of his work also involves the computer, but after losing untold hours online reading about baseball statistics and obsessively hitting the "get mail" button, Milstein decided it was time for some order, and a schedule.

A cornerstone of his system is getting out to a local coffee shop each morning, where the semi-public space and white noise help him to focus. He also builds in a certain amount of goofing-off time every day, when he's allowed to watch television or just lie on the couch and read a book. Giving himself license not to get any work done at certain parts of the day was a huge step in his becoming more productive, especially because he's usually working nights as well. His schedule varies, but according to Milstein, some variation of the following is the weekday standard:

8 a.m.: Head to the cafe, where a big cup of coffee fuels the next several hours of intense working time. The first hour is spent going through a hailstorm of e-mails about theater matters—scheduling rehearsals and logistics, communicating with the press, working with designers, and managing everyone's mini dramas. Check out the baseball scores, read the morning news, answer personal e-mails. I end up with a very fuzzy line between the personal and the various kinds of work. It's all personal, sort of. That's part of what keeps me charged up, and part of what I enjoy. I tend to think more about dealing with the outside world versus dealing with the abstract world.

10 a.m.: Shift to the programming work for a focused few hours. The caffeine-induced sense of omnipotence is at its peak and I feel excited about tackling the interesting problems of programming. I'm happily solving problems, adding features to the system, fixing bugs, and the like. When I'm in this sort of programming binge, I enjoy the calmness of not dealing with anyone else. The music is turned up loud on my headphones, and it's very satisfying.

2 p.m.–6 p.m.: Head home to have lunch and read the paper. Recognizing that I never get any good work done in the semi-groggy post-lunch part of the day, this is the time to take a nap. Read a book. Run an errand. Deal with phone calls. Take the dog for a long walk. Squeeze in a run. Most important, the computer is off limits. I think I set up this "time off in the afternoon thing" because I was just wasting so much time online and it was making me hate myself. So now I understand that I simply don't have the willpower to have it on *all the time*, and I try to be more effective when it is on.

6:30 p.m.: Most of the year, this means heading to rehearsals. This is the social part of the day when I need to be "on" and able to lead, which is why I give myself license to goof off all afternoon. Rehearsals are a huge amount of fun, but everyone looks to me and asks "What next?" pretty much at every step. That's why it's so complementary to the morning time. I like leading things and feeling out how a group is working, and giving people precise, detailed feedback in person—all of which feels completely different from the sort of intensely abstract world of writing code.

Milstein confesses that this schedule is somewhat aspirational, as most schedules tend to be: "That's my basic plan, and it's all sort of variable. Some days I'll be at the theater at ten a.m. to pick up the keys, and the whole thing is a wash, with other things entering the mix. But it's a good basic plan so I don't have to think about how my day will work in general. As Annie Dillard says somewhere in *The Writing Life*, 'A schedule is a scaffold so you can stand and work unhindered for great blocks of time,' or something like that."

Hampe, Melcher, and Milstein used similar processes to set up a structure for a slash life. At the core of each was a healthy shot of self-awareness. Hampe knew that the only way he could keep his workaholic tendencies under control was to put himself on a reduced schedule at his corporate job. Melcher had to structure his week so that he had the necessary time and space to give to his different kinds of work. Milstein had to get out of the house with its distractions. Once they settled on some goals, each had to look at the calendar and come up with some kind of a plan, whether in increments of days, weeks, months, or quarters. Equally important, each built in a system for falling off the plan, which inevitably happens. **Rigidity has no place in a slash life.** These are but a few examples of how it can be done.

In or Out of the Closet: How and When to Reveal?

One theme that plagues a good number of slashes (especially the ones with incongruous combinations) is whether to be open about the various parts of their life in all settings. Chapter 7 touched on this in terms of thinking about your introduction and other ways of presenting yourself when meeting new people. But the issues are a little different when you are dealing with deeper relationships.

Aileen Bordman, the money manager who made a documentary film about the painter Monet's relationship with the culinary delicacies of Normandy (and launched a related line of products), says she felt she had a fiduciary duty to her clients to be up front about her new venture. "What if they stumbled on an article about Aileen Bordman, the filmmaker, in the Newark *Star-Ledger*?" She also felt that she'd be missing out on opportunities by not being open about her new business venture. "Why close off half your network?" she asks. As it turns out, one of her money management clients has expressed interest in investing in her new business.

For others, the rule of too-much-information applies. Deborah Rivera, the executive recruiter/chef/hotelier, says she is cautious about discussing her hotel and restaurant with all her corporate clients. Her recruiting work is very technical and requires such focus that she would never want a client to think she is less than fully committed. But in close relationships she does reveal her other life, and there are occasions when she brings her two worlds together. Each summer, she sponsors a table at a large charity event near the town where her hotel is located. A handful of clients always make the guest list.

Carrie Lane, the Pilates instructor/art consultant/author, follows the lead of the situation, beginning in an all-Pilates or all-art mode of interaction until the timing feels right to bring up her other life. For some of the academics or collectors she deals with in the art world, the right time to talk about Pilates is never. With her Pilates clients, her art business or academic research often comes up. "Many of my clients are collectors or just have an interest in art," she explained, "and since I'm working with them in a one-on-one setting, often several times a week, we get to know one another, which means we talk about what we're doing the rest of the day. For me, sometimes I'm heading down to the galleries in Chelsea or to a private library for research, and my clients are interested in hearing about it."

The Importance of Boundaries

Not all combinations coexist readily. Certain professions have ethics issues you need to take into account if you're thinking of adding another career to the mix. That usually doesn't mean it's not possible to slash—it just means you have to draw some lines.

Who better to talk about boundaries than a shrink? When I spoke about this with Robert Childs, the psychotherapist/violin maker, he told me that he has drawn very distinct lines between his two lives. "As a psychologist, you can't be in dual roles with the people you treat," he explained. "My patients never go up to my shop and I would never treat a patient who's been a customer. But I do work with a lot of artists, and even a few musicians, as patients." Amy Bloom, the author/psychotherapist, came to a different decision based on the nature of her practice. Different facts yield different solutions.

Journalism is another field where codes of ethics exist. The profession expects that journalists will be free from conflicts of interests with the subjects they cover, which could rule out certain business relationships. Indeed, most of the journalist slashes I interviewed had pretty clear lines and didn't find it very difficult to decide where to draw them. When Marty Munson, the health editor at *Marie Claire* magazine, got certified as a personal trainer, she ruled out working at a health club that could be covered by her magazine. "I'll be working with individual clients in private clubs to make sure there are no potential conflicts of interests," she explained. Sreenath Sreenivasan, the journalist/professor/speaker, says it's simple: he gets paid for his speeches but he would never take a dime from Google or another technology company he recommends in his lectures.

Bob Woodward, one of the most respected journalists in the country, was widely criticized during the investigation surrounding the leaked disclosure of CIA operative Valerie Plame's name to the media. Woodward kept his discussions with a journalistic source from his editors at the *Washington Post*. His sin, as described by the *New York Times*: "It's the second time this year that Mr. Woodward's loyalties to a book seemed to cross with his duty to his newspaper."[2] His paper stood behind him, but many commentators questioned whether his role as an author compromised his duty to the readers of his newspaper.

On the other hand, consider the story of Dr. Sanjay Gupta, who took some flak in journalistic circles by stepping over the line from objective reporter to participant in a news story when he performed emergency surgery on a number of patients during the war in Iraq. Gupta and CNN took the position that humanity comes before the artificial constraints of the journalistic profession.

One lawyer/literary agent I spoke to said that she has to make sure, before taking on a client either as an agent or a lawyer, that she doesn't have another representation that could present a conflict of interest. For example, she could not represent an author in a dispute with a publisher she deals with in her agent role. She doesn't see this as an obstacle, but it is something she keeps in mind whenever taking on a new client.

Keeping a blog, an online diary, has been known to get some folks in trouble (or perceived trouble) with their employers. Disclosing confidential information about your employer, bad mouthing your company, or posting inappropriate photos online are good ways to ensure you won't have a job (other than your blogging) for too much longer.

Taking too much time off from a job to pursue a slash is another minefield. According to an article in the *New York Times*, high school teacher Matthew Kaye lost his teaching job when he took a few too many personal days to compete on the professional wrestling circuit (where he had a persona based on his background as a teacher).[3] Remember, if you're moonlighting, it's always a good idea to keep your daylight employer happy.

If you have a footing in one field and are considering getting into another, make sure to give some thought as to whether your profession has any codes of ethics that would prohibit what you're considering doing. While you're thinking about these issues, review "Moonlighting Dos and Don'ts" in chapter 8.

GETTING TO SLASH / / / / /

- Many slashes create a work/life that suits them so well that it doesn't feel like "work." Even though they often put in long hours, they tend to say that they do not feel overworked.

- Anticipate the inevitable conflicts among your various slashes and develop systems to keep yourself covered. Stay on top of your schedule. Delegate when possible. Build relationships with colleagues who can cover for you in crunch times.

- Develop techniques to improve your focus.

- Identify scraps of time or idle moments in your life and see if you can put them to good use.

- Check in with yourself from time to time to see how things are going and whether the current mix of activities is still working. Recognize and expect that you will need to tweak things periodically.

- Think about whether there are any potential conflicts among the various slashes you are pursuing. Ask yourself whether there are any ethical issues, duties to clients, or other considerations you need to address. ▪

CHAPTER 10 / SPECIAL CONSIDERATIONS OF PARENT SLASHES

After my first child, I couldn't help thinking, "What's a mother? What am I doing?" I felt like I needed something else. I was just the big breast. I felt so conflicted. I knew how valuable mothers were—had made films on that subject—yet I couldn't be just a mother. Part of why I work is that I have a son and a daughter and I feel it's a good example for them to see me work. Part of it is that I'm just so driven. Plus, I've never been able to define myself as just one thing.

> —Mary Mazzio, mother/Olympic rower-turned-lawyer/filmmaker

But I love my kids
so much more
than I planned.

> —Allison in the play *Eve-olution*, by Hilary Illick and Jennifer Krier

Parenting is different from other slashes. Having a child isn't a career, a vocation, or an avocation. Rather, it is a transformative life event, full-time, permanent, unpaid, and ever changing. Yet when I talked with people about the subject of slash lives, they often asked me how parenting fits in. Since, by definition, everyone who becomes a parent is a slash—blending parenting with all their other identities—the subject is certainly worth exploring.

That said, the issue of combining parenting with other career paths is one that has filled the pages of many books. This chapter is not meant as a replacement for those books, nor does it take a position on anyone's choices about how to parent or whether to become one. Instead, it is meant to highlight some of the ways people have created lives that blend parenting with gratifying careers. Like the earlier chapters, it also offers advice from those who have overcome obstacles and highlights some of the synergies that exist between parenting and other work.

Even those who are predisposed to slash careers say that once they added "parent" to the mix, it became difficult, at least initially, to pursue as many things as vigorously as they had done before. When I interviewed parents, that truth revealed itself in myriad ways. It's also the reason that many of the people featured in this book had no children at the time they were cultivating their slash lives. Some made room for children later in life; some stepped up multiple career paths after their children were in school or grown; and others will likely not have children.

Becoming a parent is also often the impetus for a career adjustment or reevaluation, especially for those who take maternity or paternity leave and have a built-in time for reflection about the state of their working lives.

As a culture, we are still at a place where blending meaningful work with parenting is not easily accomplished. When the combination coexists successfully, it is often because people have crafted a life that honors who they want to be as a parent as well as whatever else they need and want to do in their life.

If you're reading this chapter, you are probably considering how to meld parenting with some other identity and wondering how others have found satisfying solutions. Maybe you already have a slash career and are wondering whether you'll have to give something up in order to be a parent. Or perhaps you're already a parent-slash-something, and want to do it a bit better. This chapter will give you some ideas.

/ / /

In the opening episode of the second season of *Desperate House-wives*, Lynette (Felicity Huffman's character) is interviewing for a high-level job in advertising after a seven-year hiatus at home with her four children. Her husband has decided it's his turn to be a stay-at-home parent. Lynette manages to ace the first interview after she convinces the hostile interviewer (who tells Lynette that she opted not to have children so that she wouldn't be derailed from her career) that her children will not be a distraction if she takes this job.

"You'll have to drag me out of here kicking and screaming," she says, explaining that being at the office with adults—who don't throw boogers against the wall and who engage in adult conversation—will be a break from the chaos at home. The interviewer tells Lynette there will be one more round and that Lynette would be wise to show up early for the following day's interview. The next scene takes place on the morning of Lynette's interview. Her husband is lying flat on the ground, writhing in pain having thrown out his back. She knows she can't leave her youngest child, still in diapers, with him. And in light of the interviewer's comment, she can't reschedule.

With no time to even make a phone call for emergency babysitting, she scoops the toddler out of the crib and heads off to the interview. At the office, she literally drops the baby off with the bemused male receptionist, with a cursory, "You love babies, right?"

The next scene takes place in a glass-walled office. The shrew from the day before and a senior-level man who's presumably making the hiring decision ask Lynette questions. Out of the corner of her eye, she sees her child teetering on the edge of the receptionist's desk, with the receptionist paying no attention. She begins to blather, then asks to be excused for a minute. Both interviewers are confused. Lynette returns moments later with a crying baby in her arms.

"Watch me multitask," she says as she changes the diaper while racing through a well-thought-out monologue about what's wrong with the agency's image (not enough awards and public service, and clients expect those things) and its Web site (too hard to navigate, no site map, etc.). The man is impressed and tells her she's hired before he rushes off to catch a flight. The shrew recoils. In celebration, Lynette throws the soiled diaper against the wall while the bitter woman stares in disbelief. The scene closes with Lynette saying, "Of course, I'll clean that up."

Over the top as it is, the scene works because it resonates on many levels. We have no doubt Lynette deserves the job. She's got the smarts and the experience. It also seems clear that Lynette will excel at work despite the inevitable crises that will arise from her being the mother of four children. And whatever happens, she certainly won't be pretending that her kids don't exist. They are as much a part of her resume as her academic credentials and the prior positions she's held. The fact that we're seeing this on *Desperate Housewives* tells us that we are past the point of shock at seeing a senior executive who's also a mom (or a mom who's also a senior executive). The fact that her husband is manning the homefront and a male receptionist is at the office are more signs that defying stereotypes about family and professional roles is ready for prime time.

After watching that episode, I called Deborah Epstein Henry, the work/life expert, to ask how she'd advise Lynette to manage her new dance between home and office life. Henry built a successful legal career while raising three young children and now, through her company Flex-Time Lawyers, counsels thousands of others on the nuances of balancing professional careers and parenting. Once we got the issue of the show's exaggeration for dramatic purposes out of the way, Henry agreed with me that the episode raised a number of important issues.

1. Figure Out Your Childcare and Your Backup Childcare.

According to Henry, the most important piece in being successful at work outside the home while raising children is to get the proper childcare in place. Proper childcare includes layers of backup, including emergency childcare in the form of: (1) your spouse or partner, if you have one; (2) available friends and family members in your community; (3) arrangements with other working parents or their nannies or babysitters to share childcare when needed; or (4) a relationship with an emergency childcare facility. In Henry's case, a flexible babysitter—an older woman with grandchildren of her own—was the ideal backup. For people in professional positions who can afford it (and who want to advance in their careers), Henry counsels having childcare available even on your "off" days for spillover situations.

2. Set Up Your Home Life in a Way That Supports Your Work Life.

Henry says that this *Desperate Housewives* episode reminded her of countless conversations she has had with members of her group who have working spouses and the importance of good communication with your partner. "One issue I hear all the time from working mothers who have partners who also work is the game you play when it's a snow day and you hit that moment of truth when you have to figure out the importance of your days' responsibilities relative to each other and fairly negotiate who gets to go to work that day." In those instances, says Henry, many people make a mistake in the heat of the moment and tend to focus on who makes more money. Her advice: focus on who has more flexibility on that particular day. If both people have crazy days and there are no emergency options, divvy up the day with one going in early and one staying late. Any bigger issues, like rethinking childcare arrangements, can be resolved after the crisis has passed.

3. Bring All of You to Work, but Know Where to Draw the Line.

"In the eighties, when women were making strides, it was about trying to conform to the male depiction of what success was. Today, we as women acknowledge our femininity more and use it to differentiate ourselves," says Henry. "This fits in with a trend I'm seeing with employers recognizing the whole person more."

Of course, there are limits to the amount of your parent-self you might want to bring to the office, and Henry cautions against emulating Lynette and replaying the whole diaper-changing-and-throwing scene in your office. "I would recommend sharing information about your life to the extent you think a colleague or client would relate or learn from your experiences," says Henry. This is really no different from the rule of too-much-information in all slash contexts. Who wouldn't benefit from having a good filter for when to stick to work-talk and when it's okay to get personal?

4. Parenting Skills Are Transferable.

Lynnette's line about multitasking is one of the more farcical moments of the episode, but Henry agrees that the analogy is rooted in reality. There's no denying that employers are starting to recognize that parenting skills are transferable to the workplace. Ann Crittenden's *If You've Raised Kids, You Can Manage Anything* convincingly argues that the very skills that are necessary to be a good parent—multitasking, functioning amid distractions, dealing with difficult people, operating with a sense of fair play and integrity—are exactly the skills needed to succeed in the world of work.

Being a parent can also be an asset in many work situations. Henry says the fact that she is a parent has been useful to her law firm in so many ways. She has brought in business through relationships in her community, deepened client relationships through a shared connection over being a parent, and learned volumes about dealing with and managing all kinds of people.

5. It's All About Economics.

Henry's last bit of advice is never to take for granted that a workplace is family-friendly just because it's the nice thing for a company to do. In the end, it's about business. "If the employee thinks about a flexible working arrangement as an entitlement, or if an employer thinks of it as a charitable arrangement, it will never be successful for anyone," she says. "The threshold question for anyone wanting this sort of balance is 'Are they talented enough that it is in an employer's financial interest to hire or retain them?' and if the answer to that question is yes, then the next step is putting the logistics into place to ensure that it's a win-win for everyone."

Henry's comments (as well as the advice in chapter 8 about negotiating an alternative schedule) are worth considering for anyone—male or female, married or single—seeking to balance family responsibilities with a professional-level job. But that route is only one option of many.

/ / /

Sometimes the best answer to the work/family conundrum is to ditch the job altogether and go the entrepreneurial route, removing an employer from the equation. So many working mothers have gone down this path that a new word, "Mompreneur," has entered the lexicon of work (and been trademarked by the authors of a series of books on mother-founded home-based businesses). This excerpt from an article in *BusinessWeek* gives a glimpse of just one sliver of home-based entrepreneurs, those setting up shop on eBay:

> Today, upwards of 430,000 people in the U.S. alone—more than are employed worldwide by General Electric Co. and Procter & Gamble combined—earn a full- or part-time living on eBay selling everything from fashion to farm equipment, with the highest sellers grossing up to $1 million a month. Of the estimated 48% of these sellers who are women, many are "mompreneurs"—corporate dropouts who have found in eBay a way to tap into an international marketplace from their kitchen tables and finesse a saner work/life balance at the same time. . . . It's no coincidence that the rise of the eBay mompreneurs comes as more highly educated women are choosing to stay at home with young children. The percentage of working women with children under the age of one dropped from a record 59% in 1998 to 55% in 2002, after rising steadily for 30 years. Some see the decrease as a referendum on the work/life balance. As in, it doesn't exist.[1]

For Debra Dicker Cohen, thirty-eight, being a stay-at-home mom was integral to the success of her business, a referral network that homeowners use to find contractors for home repair projects. "When I pitched my story to local press, I explained I was a stay-at-home mom looking for a balance between work and family," Cohen wrote in the manual she sells to others wanting to replicate her business formula. She leveraged parenting as a way to build her own business by (1) reaching out to other stay-at-home parents looking for work that could be done from home; and (2) pitching herself to the media as a Mompreneur. (Cohen was profiled in one of the Mompreneur books.) She succeeded because her business never required her to compromise or hide her role as a parent.

After struggling over leaving her children behind for yet another business trip for her previous job, Cohen decided it was time to "retire" to the suburbs to care for her infant daughter full-time. Before long, she was battling both boredom and financial pressure. Her prior work had given her a glamorous lifestyle, including frequent travel throughout Latin America. After leaving the job, she and her husband were struggling to manage a house they had bought as a dual-income couple on his income as a teacher. Cohen was drifting and depressed. She knew she had to do something about it.

Around this time, she was settling into a new neighborhood and muddling through a series of home repairs. When it took three different exterminators to tackle a recurring rodent problem in her attic, she realized there was a business opportunity in matching homeowners with reliable contractors. It was a simple idea and she knew it would take off. Cohen started her business in 1997 with a $5,000 loan against her husband's retirement fund; within six months she had paid that back and made a profit.

She has never used outside childcare, doing the bulk of her work during her children's naps and during weekends and evenings when they were small. Once the children were in school, her husband, Charlie, a high school teacher, coached sports teams in the afternoons until Cohen's business was profitable enough for him to quit. After he gave up his slash jobs, he was able to be home in the afternoons and on Saturdays to watch the children.

Cohen handled all of her own public relations, and with each press mention she was flooded with phone calls—from contractors who wanted to be part of the network, and from homeowners who wanted to sign up for the service. But most of the calls came from people in other locales who wanted to know how to get a similar business going in their neighborhoods. Cohen knew it was time to expand. After working with a small-business consultant, she decided to write up her business plan and sell it, along with some private sessions with her, as a "business in a box." By the end of 2005 her revenues topped $2 million and she had sold more than 500 business packages. She also markets a database program she created to help her clients manage their referral businesses.

Cohen achieved all this without leaving her home for more than a few hours at a time, something that is integral to how she wants to parent. She steadfastly avoided conferences or meetings that would take her away from home. Instead, her strategy was to grow her business by aggressively courting the print media and building her network via the phone and Internet.

My interview with Cohen took place at her "summer office," a pastel blue beach club on the Long Island Sound where she works Memorial Day through Labor Day, forwarding phone calls to her cell phone. Work and life are completely integrated. At her beach club cabana, which she shares with another family, she idles away the summer days with other moms whose kids are occupied at the club's camp.

Now that Cohen's business has provided them with financial stability, Charlie is building his own entrepreneurial venture. Along with two partners, he launched the Long Island Golf Academy, a six-week golf instruction program that marries his two passions—coaching and golf. He still teaches during the school years, but he has given up working at camps and other jobs he used to take over the summer.

Cohen is not unusual in changing the parameters of a career after having children. Like so many slashes who blend multiple vocations into a unified life, Cohen has been able to do that with her business and her parenting. She has also capitalized on the synergies between her two roles: being a parent helps her relate to her clients and the representatives who buy her business packages, many of whom also spend their days at home dealing with house maintenance and small children underfoot. Whether on the phone with a contractor, a homeowner, or one of her fellow home referral entrepreneurs, Cohen never hides the fact that she works from home, and at any time her two children could be creating background noise. She's also created a life in which talking with other mothers about the challenges of juggling work and family is part of her daily diet. **The idea of creating a working life that fits around the way you want to parent is a common attitude among satisfied slash parents.**

/ / /

S. Mitra Kalita, twenty-nine, an author/journalist, was very focused on her career through her mid-twenties. After attending the Graduate School of Journalism at Columbia University, she went on to a series of jobs as a reporter at various newspapers and eventually landed at the *Washington Post* on the metro staff, which was filled with "young hungry people who were the best thing wherever they were before." At the same time, she was finishing up her first book, *Suburban Sahibs*, a nonfiction exploration of the relationship between immigrant communities and the suburbs. Kalita was proving herself at the paper, breaking stories that were well-received, when suddenly her life took an unexpected turn.

About a year into her time at the *Post*, Kalita learned she was pregnant. She asked for and was granted six months' maternity leave, but even though she was on a fast-track career path, she doubted she would want to go back to work at the end of the leave. "I just didn't see any women around me who were juggling it all very well and when I saw them at their desks at 9 p.m., I secretly thought, 'I don't want that life.'" She had also grown up with a stay-at-home mom and appreciated having had someone who was always there and a home that was the hub of all activity.

Kalita's daughter Naya was born a few weeks early and when she was in the hospital, she missed a deadline for an article she was writing freelance for a magazine. When the editor called her, Kalita was in the hospital. She took the call, explained where she was, but still finished the article within three days of giving birth. "I just didn't want to let anyone down," she explained. "And even three days into it, I realized my whole illusion of being a stay-at-home mom was not an [acceptable] reality. I thrive on having multiple things going on. It just gives me a whole lot of satisfaction to be a woman who can do it all—maybe not at the same time, but in the same week. So writing that piece was a sign of things to come."

Six weeks later, Kalita traveled with her newborn to New York's Chinatown to accept an award. Her parents and husband accompanied her, along with the breast pump and stroller, and she realized that she was not going to be able to retire her reporter's identity because she had become a mother. Kalita's work focuses on immigrant communities and families, and having a child made her feel even more connected to the issues she was writing about. "I couldn't give up writing about these kinds of things because they mattered even more now that I had a child," she told me.

Kalita did make a few changes to the way she worked. When she returned to her job at the paper, it was on a part-time schedule, leaving two days a week for her own writing and to be at home with Naya. By going part-time after establishing her value to the paper, Kalita has been able to jump out of the rat race and actually live a real community-based life, something that informs her writing while allowing her to be more integrated in her daughter's life. As she put it, "I decided that my work would be more profound than prolific and that I would try to make every story I write really count. And even when I'm in playgroup, I now find stories there, talking with other mothers, just existing as a human being."

Kalita's husband, Mukul, an art director/artist/DJ, has also made some changes to his working life since having Naya. He still divides his time between his day job as an art director and his fine art, but late nights as a DJ have largely disappeared. He has also given up a lot of social things, like just hanging around with other artists. But, he says, he now focuses on making art rather than being part of any particular art scene. Whereas he used to play drums in a band, now he plays with Naya and is looking for a music class to do with her. Kalita and Mukul work with their muses—his art and music, her books—in the evening hours when Naya is asleep and on weekends when they cover for each other. **Reorienting the way you pursue your interests and/or work—or pursuing them in a way that includes time with your child—is a smart strategy that many parents employ to make sure they don't lose their passions when they become parents.**

During the week, Kalita and Mukul take a slash approach to childcare, using a variety of arrangements. "When I was pregnant everyone said consistency was best, but we have a child who thrives on being in different environments," says Kalita. On Tuesdays and Thursdays a nanny whom they share with another family comes to the house to care for Naya while Kalita works at home. On Wednesdays, Mukul takes Naya to a day care center near his office. "Those days he's in charge," Kalita said. On Mondays and Fridays, Naya is either with Kalita or at the home of a Salvadoran woman who is a flexible babysitter as well as a part of the couple's extended family.

The family is now looking for a new home, having outgrown the starter Cape Cod they settled in when Naya was born. The new home will have room for Mukul's drum set, which was stored in the basement when Naya was born. "Everyone says you'll never be the same after having children," says Kalita, "and sure, the 3 a.m. thing is really hard. But we've realized that Naya hasn't stopped us from being us. In fact, she has strengthened a lot of our interests. Some things, like his drumming, may sound like hobbies, but they are really our definition of ourselves so they cannot be relegated to the basement."

Kalita and Mukul have found it relatively easy to fold their new identities as parents into the lives they were already living. Though they made changes to the way they lived after Naya was born, Kalita says that what struck her most was how little she felt she had to give up in order to raise Naya the way she wanted to. Like Deborah Epstein Henry, the lawyer who talks about how her children's network helps her bring in clients, Kalita learned that being a mother has deepened her commitment to the issues she is interested in writing about. Of course, with a couple there are twice as many ways to tinker with both the logistics of home and the logistics of work, and Kalita and Mukul's story shows that as well.

Kalita and Mukul were both raised by Indian parents, and exposing Naya to cross-cultural experiences—in their community, in her childcare, and in both her parents' working lives—is an important part of how they want to parent. In today's world, Kalita says that children aren't integrated enough into parents' multiple lives. Still, she concedes it's a little easier for them than for other parents. "It's easier to take a kid to an art opening than to a meeting of investment bankers."

/ / /

At thirty-one, Jennifer Krier had the job opportunity she had always dreamed of. After obtaining a Ph.D. in anthropology with a focus on gender and power in matrilineal societies, she got a tenure-track position at Cornell University in Ithaca, New York. She was married with two young children when she accepted the job; her husband had his own career in business in Boston. Though they knew it would be hard on the family, the couple decided to commute between Boston and Ithaca so that each of them could pursue their careers. The children stayed in Ithaca with Krier, where they spent their days in day care or with an au pair, and Krier's husband joined them on the week-ends. In the summers they all lived together in Boston.

Their careers may have been on track, but family life was chaos. "My life was counting the days until Thursday nights when we'd be together, constantly packing all of our belongings, and transitioning the kids to new childcare situations. It was totally dismal, like a gray Ithaca morning," said Krier of that period. After three years of this, Krier began to question whether the academic career she was striving for even made sense now that she had a husband (whose work was tied to Boston) and two children. "It all started to seem unrealistic," she told me. "What was I going to do—go back to Indonesia with my two babies and a husband who doesn't like third-world travel?"

She took a two-year leave of absence and decided to move back to Boston so the family could live in one place and she could make some order out of her life. She took a carrel in the library, put her kids in day care, and began to work on a book. She also did a lot of reflecting. "At first I thought I'd be taking a few years off and then get into the academic scene in Boston. But then I realized that academia wasn't who I was on an authentic level. Teaching and working in an office was one thing, but there was also the pressure of all those outside projects. Also, the culture of academia is very competitive, with a lot of posturing and politicking, which I wasn't good at. There just isn't a lot of joy in it and it wasn't me," she explained. "Plus, my husband had an eighty-hour-a-week job and I couldn't face having kids and not being with them."

Krier was going through a classic mid-career reassessment, questioning whether the career she had chosen a decade earlier was living up to her expectations. In her case, the issue was complicated by the fact that she also had other responsibilities competing for her attention and focus.

Krier decided not to go back to Cornell and instead settled into suburbia, where she encountered her next struggle—what kind of mother to be. She couldn't identify with mothers who were home all day with their children; yet the career she had been striving for didn't feel right either. Peace of mind came in the form of a friendship with Hilary Illick, a mother/writer Krier met in a Mommy & Me gymnastics class.

In Illick, Krier discovered an outlet for some of her darkest confessions about modern motherhood. After hours of frank discussions about their guilt about being bad mothers, their professional disappointments, even their sexual mishaps, the two soon realized they had the makings of a creative work that would speak to others. They decided to meet for daily writing sessions, following the "morning pages" model of Julia Cameron's book, *The Artist's Way*. At the beginning, they just started recording their conversations in journals, having no idea what they were doing.

Less than a year after starting those morning pages, those confessional monologues became the basis of a play, at first titled *Venus de Minivan*, which they performed themselves as a reading at a yoga studio. "Basically, we took our lives as they existed and turned them into art," says Krier. "As an academic I felt like I had to pretend that parenting didn't take anything out of me. So it was such a relief to write that play, which was about how parenting completely reoriented me." Several months later, using some connections they had in the literary world, the script was optioned and Krier and Illick rewrote it under a new name, *Eve-olution*, which opened off-Broadway to enormous acclaim with professional actors playing the two writer/moms. The writers had no idea their little creative project would end up reaching such a wide audience.

When I met Krier in the summer of 2005, she was in the midst of yet another transition. She was finishing up training to be a life coach, a field that she says is the ideal complement to motherhood. "With coaching, the time that I have to be on call for a client is so short, usually forty-five minutes," she reflected. "Even with a kid home sick I can stick them in front of the television for forty-five minutes. It's about using all the resources I already have as a human being to help someone else come into awareness. As an academic you have to do all this research and be the expert. In coaching, the client is the expert, the expert in his life. It's so much about what's happening in the moment. As a parent you have to dance in the moment all the time, you have to improvise, be spontaneous, come up with new solutions, and those are the kinds of skills coaching taps into."

Coaching has a relationship to her anthropology work as well. "Instead of studying lots of people from one culture, I now study one person at a time, along with their own inner culture." Krier says it's hard to peel back the layers of her different identities. Motherhood turned her into a playwright and her play examined motherhood as an anthropologist might. "That play is really the ethnography of everyday suburban life for someone in my gender and culture, of my class and race."

In typical slash fashion, what sounds like an unlikely collection of ingredients has simmered together to create a well-blended stew. Even so, Krier realizes that the recipe may need to change again. Following her heart is a skill that will help her stay on top of that. As with all slash pairings, what matters is that it's working for her at the moment. For parents, this might even be more true than for any other slashes, since parenthood and what it requires of you by definition evolves over time.

/ / /

Krier evolved into her post-parent career path because what she was doing before didn't feel right anymore. Another approach is to build a career from the ground up with the plan of blending parenting into it.

Amy Salzhauer started Ignition Ventures (along with co-founder Maureen Stancik Boyce) with the specific goal of creating a family-friendly environment. A business in which almost no one works full-time and work is done on a project basis was the solution. Salzhauer came to Ignition after a slash career with stints as an environmentalist, journalist, consultant, and scientist, often with overlapping periods.

When I interviewed Salzhauer, she was on maternity leave from her own company and nursing a five-month-old daughter. She was in the process of figuring out how she would return to her position as CEO on a part-time basis. She plans to have a crib in the office and a nanny on hand. Her husband, a physician, plans to continue to work full-time, but he will likely scale down his outside activities.

Salzhauer echoed a view I heard a lot when speaking to high-achieving types, mostly women, who were finding their way as parents—that they are willing to reorganize their chosen careers to make room for parenting responsibilities. Before children,

Salzhauer was the model fast-tracker who'd made it onto some of those 40-under-40 business achiever lists that magazines like to run. But from the start, she wanted to build the kind of company that would allow her to have children. She was also determined to create an environment for others—employees and independent contractors—who wanted to live the same way. Company planning meetings involve a lot of talk about goals and Salzhauer says money isn't usually high on the list. "A top goal for the year could be making sure that a person who is having a child doesn't travel. Or that someone needs to spend more time outdoors. Or to take projects that have a positive impact on the world. Money is often something like twenty-one on the list," she explained.

Salzhauer acknowledges that there are tradeoffs, primarily on the revenues front, but being a private company gives Ignition the ability to think like this. Her advice to others: "You can pay attention to salary, you can pay attention to work/life, and you can pay attention to both. But you might have to give up something to get something."

/ / /

While they are still considered pioneers, a small but growing number of men are scaling down their careers to make more time for parenting or to allow their partners to pursue a demanding career.

Sally Hogshead, the advertising executive/author, has two young children. Her husband, Rich Johnson, is a stay-at-home dad. They came to that arrangement for a few reasons. Johnson is twelve years older than Hogshead and was in a good place in his career to take some time off, whereas Hogshead was running her own advertising agency and was nowhere near wanting to take time out. As a couple, they decided that Johnson would take to the role of stay-at-home parent whereas Hogshead says she is a better parent when she can also engage with other goals.

Even with a husband assuming a lot of the daily jobs of parenting, Hogshead says that combining career and family is challenging. "Basically, our situation works about as well for us as the traditional roles work for other couples. In other words, it's hard, but no harder. The difficulty has less to do with gender and more to do with the fact that it's tough for any two people to juggle work and family responsibilities. Marriage and raising kids are hard, for any couple. It's wonderful and joyful and amazing . . . and hard."

While this arrangement solves a lot of business concerns for Hogshead, it results in a lot of bewildered reactions for her husband. "Once in a while he gets asked what else he does," she said. "People are still not entirely ready for a father with no other slashes. People sometimes have the perception that he somehow ended up in this position, as though he didn't have a choice. Nothing could be further from the truth. He retired from one job, in advertising, and embarked on the next, as a dad."

/ / /

Bonnie Duncan, the teacher/dancer/puppeteer, and Dan Milstein, the computer programmer/theater director, are talking a lot these days about fitting parenthood into an already slash-filled household. They expect that they will each do some reshuffling, especially in the near term.

Duncan has thought a lot about how having a child will fit in with being a dancer. "The dancing I do is all acrobatic with a certain amount of danger to it, so it's just not something I can do if I'm pregnant," she explained. "And to be in the right physical shape, I would have to miss some time performing." She expects to get back to her dancing as soon as her body allows.

That said, her teaching and puppetry are things she plans to continue without much of a break.

A lot of their planning has to do with logistics, Duncan told me. "With the way my teaching works, I work one to two days a week (say, from 9 to 1 p.m. or so) and sometimes I work just one morning a week in a school. Either way, I can take on as much work as I need (as long as arts funding is around). I figure that would be about right if I have a small child at home. Alternatively, Dan seems to work on his computer from 9 to 2 p.m. as well. I assume that we'd be able to juggle who is at home and who is out of the house—this is where the flexibility of our careers is great. We have talked a lot about how important it is to make sure we both get to do our artist work as much as we can."

Milstein is evaluating his own slash mix as well, and he's assuming he will have to scale back across the board. "It's even possible that I won't be able to make Rough & Tumble [his theater company] work anymore, though I think I'll be able to find a way to keep it going in some form," he explained. "The computer gig definitely provides us with a level of security. And I feel very, very lucky that there is something I find interesting and challenging that is lucrative enough so that I can do it part-time and make a living. Very, very lucky. The ratio will shift when/if we have a family, but I'll still do lots of things that interest and challenge me."

The fact that Milstein and Duncan have each cultivated so many professional paths gives them options and more flexibility than most people. Of course, as S. Mitra Kalita's story shows, no one knows what kind of parent they will end up wanting to be, but having a flexible life already in place provides a lot of options. Once you have the foundation, it's up to you to build the life that makes sense for you, *at any given time.*

DON'T GO IT ALONE //////

Support groups for working mothers (and increasingly, fathers) are the new networking meccas. During working lunches and in online discussion groups, parents who split their time between a career and child rearing trade tips on everything from nanny nuisances to face-time frustration (at the office, of course). Most of these resources are directed toward mothers, but fathers who have taken on a lot of childcare responsibilities may relate to the issues under discussion (and will often get a warm welcome at meetings). If parenting and work has the distinction of being one of the most challenging slash combinations, it is also one of the most universal ones, which means that support is available. Why not learn from others who are facing the same issues? Here are a few resources that can help.

On the Web:

- Catalyst (www.catalyst.org)
- Families and Work Institute (www.familiesandwork.org)
- Mompreneurs Online (www.mompreneursonline.com)
- Mothers & More (www.mothersandmore.org)
- National Council of Women's Organizations (www.womensorganizations.org)
- Slowlane (www.slowlane.com)—a resource for stay-at-home fathers, including those working at home.
- Women Working 2000 + Beyond (www.womenworking2000.com)
- Work+Life Fit, Inc. (www.workpluslife.com)
- *Working Mother* magazine and Web site (www.working mother.com)

Books:

- Ann Crittenden, *If You've Raised Kids, You Can Manage Anything: Leadership Begins at Home* (New York: Gotham Books/ Penguin Group, 2004).
- Linda Mason, *The Working Mother's Guide to Life: Strategies, Secrets, and Solutions* (New York: Three Rivers Press, 2002).

- Ellen Parlapiano and Patricia Cobe, *Mompreneurs: A Mother's Practical Step-by-Step Guide to Work-at-Home Success* (New York: Perigee, 1996); and *Mompreneurs Online: Using the Internet to Build Work@Home Success* (New York: Perigee, 2001).

- Mary W. Quigley and Loretta E. Kaufman, *Going Back to Work: A Survival Guide for Comeback Moms* (New York: St. Martin's Griffin, 2004).

- Wendy Sachs, *How She Really Does It: Secrets of Successful Stay-at-Work Moms* (New York: Da Capo Lifelong Books, 2005).

GETTING TO SLASH / / / / /

- If you're balancing parenting with work outside the home, you'll need to set up your home life in a way that supports your work life. Figure out your childcare, as well as backup childcare.

- Bring all of you to work but know where to draw the line. As is true with all slash combinations, you need to recognize the appropriate time and place to talk about or grapple with the challenges of your various responsibilities.

- Like all slash synergies, parenting provides skills that are transferable to other jobs and many opportunities to connect with others over a shared experience. Recognize parenthood as a way of forging relationships with many people with whom you'd otherwise have little in common.

- When negotiating an alternative work schedule with an employer, don't assume that a workplace is family-friendly just because it's the nice thing for a company to do. Remember that it's about business and think about why your alternative work schedule is a win-win for both you and your employer.

- Sometimes the best answer to the work/family conundrum is to ditch the job altogether and go the entrepreneurial route, removing an employer from the equation. Consider working from home, starting your own business, or forming a working life that in some other way blends easily with your role as a parent.

- The idea of creating a working life that fits around the way you want to parent is a common attitude among satisfied slash parents.

- Recognize that parenting as a couple affords twice as many ways to tinker with both the logistics of home and the logistics of work.

- Pursuing your interests in a way that includes time with your child is a smart strategy that many parents employ to make sure they don't lose their passions when they become parents.

- Like in any slash combination, the way you blend work and parenting will need to be tinkered with over time as your career opportunities and the needs of your family evolve. ■

EPILOGUE / / / / /

Europeans, who take four-to-six-week annual holidays while also managing to have jobs and families, seem to come naturally to work/life balance. Yet somehow Americans can't seem to get it right.

I used to think it was all about boundaries—about turning off the cell phone, leaving work at the office, and making time for vacations. I now think it's just the opposite, that it's not about respecting boundaries at all, but rather about letting your various vocations and identities commingle so that it's sometimes hard to tell when you're working and when you're just living.

It's ironic that it took me so long to figure this out. For a big chunk of my childhood, my family lived above a motel that my parents owned. In those years, there was no separation between work and the rest of our lives. Dinner was routinely interrupted by the ring of the buzzer downstairs, beckoning one of us to answer the call and take twenty minutes to check in a guest or deal with an overflowing toilet. Once the night clerk arrived, we were technically free, but my father and mother were never really off duty. A guest could have a health emergency or the night clerk could turn out to have a drinking problem, and suddenly they were back in work mode.

When my parents socialized, they did it at home by hosting dinner parties or poker games, never venturing too far from the business. Friends and family pitched in at the front desk. If company visited, I took them across the street to the beach. And when my mom had an errand for me, I came back from the beach and ran to the store in my bathing suit and flip-flops. When I needed a haircut, my father broke out his scissors in the kitchen and propped me up on the counter by the sink; he had been a hairdresser for twenty years and in our household he never gave up that role. I was about twenty-five when I had my first haircut by a stranger (by then they were called hair stylists). Now that I think of it, the social part of our lives was indistinguishable from the work. The staff and guests at our motels were just the people who populated our life.

When I graduated from college, I was determined to have a job I could walk away from at the end of the day, so I went to law school. For nearly a decade, I worked as a corporate lawyer in the kind of life I thought I wanted. When I left the office, even if it was late, I left the work behind, and then my personal life began. For a while this worked, but soon I felt like I had one identity at work and another one the moment I left the office. I didn't feel integrated at all. The moments of real pleasure I experienced at work were when I let parts of my outside life seep in, like when I used the perks of corporate life to feed my travel itch. I planned trips for my bosses, hosted international colleagues, and raised my hand for conferences and out-of-town meetings. Whenever I did these things, my life felt more integrated.

When I became a writer, being myself came naturally. The work I do consists of things I'd do even if no one paid me. When I travel, I often find a way to publish something about my trip. When I want to learn about something, I write an article about it. When I teach, moderate panels, or speak to groups of people, I'm often being paid to mentor, something I enjoy and do for free on a regular basis. Now, whether I'm writing, teaching, speaking, reading, or getting together with others in the world of words, I usually can't tell the difference between my work and my life.

When I talk to Angela Williams, the lawyer/minister, about this, she calls it leading an "authentic life." As she put it, "If you are in touch with who you are, willing to allow people to see you for who you really are, and willing to be really vulnerable, that's what makes you authentic and that's what allows you to bridge the gap between the personal and the community, the secular and spiritual. I have been graced with opportunity to move in a number of different settings, from prisons to boardrooms and every segment of my life is intertwined. When you weave the threads of your life together, the whole of you comes out."

Many of the people in this book live slash lives out of a desire to pursue multiple paths simultaneously. They do it to nurture competing interests, to develop diverse talents, or to satisfy an incredibly curious and restless nature. But for legions of others, there is no choice but to slash. If you're a single or working parent, for example, a slash life isn't an option, it's a necessity.

Still, in the end I believe we are all slashes by necessity. After all, who can answer the question "What do you do?" with a singular response? And why would we want to? ■

APPENDIX //////

SAMPLE SLASH BIOS, RESUMES, AND WEB SITES

On the following pages are examples of some of the creative ways slashes in the book have handled their resumes, biographies, and Web pages. The opportunities for innovative slash presentations are limitless, but these samples should give you some idea of what others have done.

Angela Williams

Angela Williams, a corporate lawyer/Baptist minister, uses both narrative and resume formats. Narratives are perfect for when she is invited to give a speech or appear at an event. Resumes are best for a job interview or for any time someone wants to get a more detailed inventory of everything she has done, in chronological order. Note that in the resume, the focus is on her legal and leadership positions, whereas her work in the church community is listed under "Community Activities and Affiliations." Her narrative bio addresses her slash in the first sentence. The bio also includes a photograph of Williams, something she decided to add because she is a frequent public speaker and is generally asked to provide a photograph along with her bio when she arranges speaking engagements.

ANGELA F. WILLIAMS
[CONTACT INFORMATION REDACTED]

SUMMARY

Proven corporate legal counselor and trial lawyer with experience in corporate compliance & ethics, complex litigation and regulatory matters. Unique expertise in non-profit management. Recognized as a motivational leader with a consistent track record in delivering bottom-line results. Effective communicator able to explain complex legal requirements to nonlawyers and provide strategic counsel to enhance business profitability. Able to establish rapport and credibility with diverse groups ranging from hourly employees to board of directors members.

*Compliance & Ethics   *Philanthropy
*Litigation and Regulatory   *Culture Change/Integration

EMPLOYMENT

BUSH-CLINTON KATRINA FUND   MARCH 2006-PRESENT
Interfaith Liaison   Washington, DC

- Responsible for understanding the overall impact of Hurricane Katrina on faith communities in Alabama, Louisiana and Mississippi. Within first two weeks, developed a grant administration process to facilitate the distribution of $20M set aside by the Fund for the rebuilding and renewal of houses of worship. Significant time devoted to monitoring, providing technical assistance and serving as program content expert for the $20M devoted to interfaith grants.

- Liaison with the Interfaith Advisory Committee appointed by President George H.W. Bush and President William J. Clinton to advise the Fund on how to best meet the needs of the faith community. Network with other organizations to coordinate support for this effort. Oversee media communications related to these grants.

SEARS, ROEBUCK & CO.   MARCH 2004-JANUARY 2006
                                                            Hoffman Estates, IL
Vice President and Deputy General Counsel, Litigation & Government Affairs   (May 2005-Jan 2006)

- As Deputy General Counsel, have ultimate responsibility for the management of all litigation with a team of 20 professionals responsible for several thousand cases. These cases range from small claims, asbestos claims, real estate disputes, premises and consumer product liability, environmental litigation, general commercial litigation, credit and financial services litigation to class actions involving wage and hour matters, Securities & Exchange Commission matters and shareholder derivative suits.

- A direct result of the merger between Sears Roebuck & Co. and Kmart Corporation, developed plan to outsource legal work and incorporated the use of litigation management tools to handle caseload with fewer Law Department staff.

- Manage the governmental affairs of the company's external lobbying firm and coordinate efforts with national and state retail associations. Manage operations of SearsPAC, a voluntary, non-profit, political action committee whose exclusive purpose is to influence the election of candidates for public office who the Committee believed would promote the protection and advancement of the retail industry.

- Chief spokesperson of the Sears/National Military Family Association partnership which funded $2 million for Operation Purple, an international summer camp program for children whose parents are deployed with the military. Attend media events and co-hosted a Capitol Hill reception with Senators Hillary Clinton and Elizabeth Dole.

Vice President and Deputy General Counsel, Chief Compliance & Ethics Officer (Mar 2004-Apr 2005)
- Managed all legal services provided to two businesses – Home Services and Credit and Financial Products with a team of 25 professionals. With revenues of approximately $2.6 billion, Home Services is the nation's largest product repair service provider with over 10,000 service technicians and over 14 million service calls annually. The Credit and Financial Products business reported revenues of over $380 million. This business includes the domestic credit card receivables portfolio and the credit protection and insurance products sold.

- A direct report to the General Counsel, CEO and Audit Committee Chair. Provided regular updates to the Audit Committee of the Board of Directors on matters related to internal investigations, ethics violations and status of the compliance program. Responsible for ensuring that ethical practices and policies were developed, embedded and enforced throughout the company. As a strategic business partner, assisted in the identification of applicable laws, regulations and other requirements to ensure that current business practices were in compliance.

- Designed and implemented company's new compliance program within first five months of employment. Developed methods for heightening employee awareness of compliance and creating an ethical environment. Achieved 100% completion of compliance program test by corporate officers and approximately 75% completion by other employees. Partnered with the Internal Audit and Finance functions to monitor remediation efforts.

BRYAN CAVE LLP   2000-2004
Attorney   Washington, D.C.
- Worked closely with clients to prevent or minimize formal charges by providing counsel and guidance during governmental investigations involving the Departments of Justice and Defense, the Internal Revenue Service and the Securities and Exchange Commission. Conducted independent investigations on behalf of boards of directors and audit committees of public companies to assist senior executives in the elimination of potentially unlawful action.

- Represented companies involving disputes alleging violations of employment discrimination statutes, shareholder derivative suits, contracts and general commercial litigation matters.

OFFICE OF SENATOR EDWARD M. KENNEDY   1998-2000
Special Counsel on Criminal Law   Washington, D.C.
- Analyzed legislative developments of specific issues; advised the Senator on initiatives critical to his Judiciary Committee legislative agenda; recommended strategies and tactics on bills and amendments; advised and assisted Majority or Minority Members during Senate floor debates, including preparation of floor statements, talking points and rebuttals to opposing argument.
- Successfully negotiated complicated and highly politicized criminal justice issues, such as the Child Protection and Sexual Predator Punishment Act, the Hate Crimes Prevention Act and the Violent Juvenile Repeat Offenders Act, by working with Democratic and Republican staff, as well as Administration and advocacy organization representatives.

DEPARTMENT OF JUSTICE, NATIONAL CHURCH ARSON TASK FORCE   1996-1998
Trial Attorney   Washington, D.C.
- Established lines of responsibility and coordinated the activities of federal agents with the Federal Bureau of Investigation and Bureau of Alcohol, Tobacco and Firearms and United States Attorney's Offices across the country.

- Successfully investigated and prosecuted approximately 25% of the federal cases nationwide involving hate crimes against and the arson of religious property.

UNITED STATES ATTORNEY'S OFFICE, MIDDLE DISTRICT OF FLORIDA   1995-1996
Assistant United States Attorney   Tampa and Orlando, FL
- As a Criminal Division attorney, responsible for prosecuting criminal referrals from federal, state and local investigative agencies. Conducted grand jury investigations and prosecuted offenses under Titles 18, 21 and 26 of the United States Code. Prosecuted seven jury trials. Briefed and argued an appeal before the United States Court of Appeals for the Eleventh Circuit.

- Investigated several arsons, complicated customs violations and various telemarketing schemes. These cases included mail fraud, wire fraud and money laundering charges.

UNITED STATES AIR FORCE   1988-1995
Assistant Staff Judge Advocate   Kansas, Republic of Korea and Washington, D.C.
- Guided management and personnel offices of the Air Force District of Washington on equal employment matters. Completely revamped flagging EEO program and developed a model for the Air Force. Provided general legal assistance to military members ranging from wills and income tax preparation to family law matters. Reviewed government contracts and advised on bid protests.

- Prosecuted nearly 100 intricate, high profile cases. Provided training in all phases of trial preparation and practice to prosecutors. An adjunct professor at the Judge Advocate General's School for Trial Advocacy.

EDUCATION
JURIS DOCTOR
University of Texas School of Law   Austin, Texas

MASTER OF DIVINITY, *cum laude*
Samuel DeWitt Proctor School of Theology, Virginia Union University   Richmond, Virginia

BACHELOR OF ARTS, American Government
University of Virginia   Charlottesville, Virginia
    Echols Scholar
    Air Force ROTC Scholarship Recipient

ADDENDUM

BAR MEMBERSHIPS
Commonwealth of Virginia
District of Columbia
State of Illinois
U.S. Court of Military Appeals
Supreme Court of the United States

PUBLICATIONS
Association of Corporate Counsel website, "What Can Bring a Billion Dollar Business Down? An Inadequate Corporate Compliance Program" (May 2003)

Association of Corporate Counsel website, "When Shredding Documents Can Lead to an Indictment" (May 2003)

United States Attorneys' Bulletin entitled "Church Arsons and Hate Crimes" (February 1998)

PROFESSIONAL ACTIVITIES AND AFFILIATIONS
American Bar Association
   Commission on Women in the Profession - Commissioner
   Litigation Section – Government Litigators Committee Co-Chair
   Young Lawyers Division – National officer (Assembly Speaker and Clerk)
   Continuing Legal Education Speaker - Trial Advocacy

Center for Work-Life Policy, Member, Hidden Brain Drain Task Force
   Research initiative co-chaired by Professors Sylvia Hewlett (Columbia University), Cornel West (Princeton University) and Carolyn Buck-Luce (Ernst & Young), focuses on how to create the conditions that allow organizations to more fully tap into the productive energies of professional women and persons of color. Findings published in the *Harvard Business Review*.
   • Member of the private sector Task Force since its inception in 2004
   • Coined phrase, "Invisible Lives," for the research around tapping the hidden strengths of minority executives
   • Quoted in several news publications about the success of minorities in corporations
   • Guest speaker at events hosted around the country by Ernst & Young on achieving success, leadership and power within a corporation
   • Guest lecturer at Columbia University on the topic of Women and Power

Henry Crown Fellow, The Aspen Institute, Class of 2005
   The Henry Crown Fellowship is designed to engage the next generation of leaders in the challenge of community-spirited leadership. It brings together young executives and professionals under the age of 45 who have already achieved conspicuous success in their chosen fields of endeavor.

COMMUNITY ACTIVITIES AND AFFILIATIONS

Christian Service Charities, President, Board of Directors (www.csoa.org)

> A federation that facilitates access and marketing in Workplace Giving Campaigns on behalf of nearly 70 Christian charities nationwide. CSC also serves as the "management consulting arm" for 3 federation partners (Medical Research Charities, Human Service Charities of America and Neighbor to Nation). On behalf of all four federation members, annual revenues total $20 million from the Combined Federal Campaign, through United Way campaigns and in state and local campaigns. For a period of seven months during 2005, served as *de facto* CEO.

angelaw Ministries (www.angelawministries.org), Founder and CEO

Bridge to Hope Ministries, Board of Directors (www.bthministry.org)

WoW 4 the Word Ministries (www.wow4theword.com), Founder and CEO

YWCA National Capital Area, Board of Directors

Angela F. Williams

Angela F. Williams is bi-vocational—she is both an ordained Baptist minister and a corporate lawyer. In 2001, the *New York Times* and *L Magazine* featured her in articles about people who pursue two full-time professions. Currently, Ms. Williams is the Interfaith Liaison for the Bush-Clinton Katrina Fund, a nonprofit organization formed to provide critically needed donations to assist the survivors of Hurricane Katrina. In this capacity, she is responsible for understanding the impact of Katrina on the faith community and overseeing the processing of $20 million in grants to rebuild houses of worship. As part of this effort, she is working with the Interfaith Advisory Committee, comprised of religious leaders appointed by Presidents Bush and Clinton and co-chaired by former Congressman William H. Gray and Bishop T.D. Jakes.

Ms. Williams recently served as Vice President and Deputy General Counsel of Litigation & Government Relations for Sears Holdings Corporation. Prior to that, she was Sears' Chief Compliance & Ethics Officer, responsible for ensuring that ethical practices and policies were developed, embedded and enforced. As the Chief of Litigation, Ms. Williams, along with a team of 20 professionals, had ultimate responsibility for the management of several thousand cases. These cases ranged from asbestos claims to real estate disputes, premises and consumer product liability, environmental litigation, general commercial litigation and class actions involving labor disputes, SEC matters and shareholder derivate suits.

As the Chief Compliance & Ethics Officer, she reported regularly to the Audit Committee of the Board, CEO and General Counsel on matters related to internal investigations, ethics violations and the status of the compliance program. She designed and implemented Sears' compliance program within her first five months of employment. As a business lawyer, she managed legal services for the $2.6 billion Home Services business and the $380 million Credit and Financial Products business.

Her legal background includes practicing law with Bryan Cave LLP, as Special Counsel on Criminal Law to Senator Edward M. Kennedy on his Senate Judiciary Committee staff, Department of Justice prosecutor with the National Church Arson Task Force, federal prosecutor in the United States Attorney's Office in the Middle District of Florida, and in the U.S. Air Force Judge Advocate General Corps.

Ms. Williams currently serves as President of the Board of Directors of Christian Service Charities (CSC) (www.christianservicecharities.org), a federation that facilitates access and marketing in Workplace Giving Campaigns on behalf of nearly 70 Christian charities nationwide. CSC also serves as the "management consulting arm" for 3 federation partners in the areas of medical research and human service charities. On behalf of all four federation members, annual revenues total $20 million from the Combined Federal Campaign, through United Way campaigns and in state and local campaigns.

She is a 2005 Henry Crown Fellow of the Aspen Institute. This program seeks to develop our next generation of community-spirited leaders, providing them with the tools necessary to meet the challenges of corporate and civic leadership in the 21st century by honing their skills in values-based leadership. Each year 20 Crown Fellows are chosen from among young executives and professionals who have already achieved considerable success in the private or public sector.

Her educational degrees include a Bachelor of Arts from the University of Virginia where she was an Echols Scholar, a Juris Doctor from the University of Texas School of Law and a Master of Divinity, *cum laude*, from the Samuel DeWitt Proctor School of Theology, Virginia Union University.

She lives in Chicago with her husband Roderick Williams, who is an Executive Director (Illinois, Iowa and Wisconsin) with Prison Fellowship.

Terence Bradford

Terence Bradford is an investment manager by day and rapper by night. As a rapper, he goes by the name Billy Shakes. The following bio of Billy Shakes appears on the Web site www.bshakes.com. It tells the story of the two worlds Bradford/Shakes travels between, and it does it in language that evokes the voice of a hip-hop artist.

Wall Street/
Hip-Hop

BILLY SHAKES: Bio

LINKS:
Homepage
Contact Us
Site Map
Search
Music Links
Investment Links
Track Listings
Updates
In the Press

You've heard this story in rap music before, right? A kid from the projects in the Bronx grows up with no dad, no money, and no hope for the future. He is sent away for 4 years, returns to the Bronx and begins to hustle on the street. He then begins a promising career in Hip-Hop. Same old story, right?

Well, not if you are talking about Billy Shakes. Shakes went away for 4 years; but not to the type of institution you are probably imagining. He went to Middlebury College, an elite liberal arts college in New England. The street on which he hustles is Wall Street, where he is an Assistant Vice President for the one of the biggest financial companies in the U.S. He also happens to be a very talented individual that can rap with the best in the business.

Billy Shakes brings Wall Street to Main Street with every verse that he spits. This is a first. Never before in the music industry has there been a recording artist who has been able to apply his unique experiences to show the connection between the stock game and the street game. Through clever rhymes, Shakes calls out the street hustlers throwing their money and lives away on cars, diamond jewelry, and guns, and shows them how they can be better spending their money. Pretty remarkable in that everyone that listens to his music will actually start learning about making money.

In "Stocks and Bonds," Shakes raps:

> Stocks and Drugs, are both the same amount in my eyes,
> More buyers than sellers causes the market to rise. . .
> I know you out there . . . click clackin' your guns,
> Hang with me, I'll have you stick stackin' mutual funds.

Then:

> Thousands on a whip (car) don't make you a star,
> I'm buying options in the company that's makin' the cars.

Through clever wordplay and bumpin' beats, Shakes demystifies the sometimes confusing world of investments to an audience largely unfamiliar with investing and saving money. After Billy Shakes is finished, the hip-hop audience will no longer fear what they do not understand, and without even realizing it, they may just learn a little something.

Bonnie Duncan

Bonnie Duncan, a dancer/teacher/puppeteer, uses a combined resume to present her various slashes. For Duncan, there is no reason to hide the various things she does, as they all complement one another nicely. As an artist, Duncan is well served by a resume that takes a creative approach to layout and design.

Bonnie Duncan

EDUCATION

Lesley University, 1999
MEd Creative Arts in Learning

New York University, 1998
"Classroom Drama in Great Britain"

Clemson University, 1997
BA Elementary Education
Magna Cum Laude
Departmental Honors

PROFESSIONAL AFFILIATIONS

Massachusetts Cultural Council
Creative Teaching Partner:
Development & Planning, Residencies
www.massculturalcouncil.org

**American Alliance for
Theatre & Education**
National Conference presenter
PreK-8 Network Project Co-Chair
Presidential Citation
www.aate.com

UNIMA-USA
published article, 2005
www.unima-usa.org

**Puppeteers of America
Boston Area Guild of Puppetry**

CONTINUED STUDIES

**Residency, Atlantic Center for the
Arts, 2005**
Associate Artist

Aerial Acrobatics, 2004-present
Gemini Trapeze, FireFlyDance, LAVA,
Ipswich Moving Company

Whirlwind's Reading in Motion, 2003
"Phonemic Awareness through Dance"

INTERESTS & SKILLS

mask making, voice work, acting,
improvisational theater, clay
sculpture, printmaking & design,
triathlon

PERFORMING ARTS EXPERIENCE

Dancer, Snappy Dance Theater, 1999-present
Collaboratively develop & perform athletic, sculptural modern dance for
national & international audiences.
www.snappydance.com

Resident Costume Designer, Rough & Tumble Theater, 1999-present
Create costume concepts & designs for award-winning theater company.
IRNE award nominee, 2003, costume design
www.rough-and-tumble.org

Puppeteer, Independent, 1999-present
Create & perform puppetry pieces for adult audiences. Performance
venues include Puppet Showplace Theater, Boston; Perishable Theater,
Providence, RI; Theatre for a New City, New York, NY. Puppet & mask
on exhibit at Revolving Museum, Lowell, MA.

Puppeteer, Luna Theatre, 2000-2002
Developed & performed shadow puppet pieces for adult audiences in
Boston area. Awarded grants from Puppeteers of America, Somerville
Arts Council, Cambridge Arts Council.
www.sarbek.com/luna

SELECTED EDUCATION EXPERIENCE

Teaching Artist, Arts in Progress, 2000-present
Develop, conduct, & assess artist residencies focused on MA Language
Arts Learning Frameworks, Boston Public Schools, grades K-7.
www.artsinprogress.org

Theater Arts Teacher, Cambridge Montessori School, 1999-2004
Created integrated curriculum for classroom studies. Led students in
creation of original plays & performances, grades 1-6.
www.cambridgemontessori.net

Director of Educational Outreach, Snappy Dance Theater, 2001-2004
Developed school assembly programs, educational materials, workshops,
& an extended residency--"Physics is a Snap". Coordinated educational
programs & performances in schools & communities nation-wide.

OTHER EXPERIENCE

Workshop Presenter, Wang Center for the Performing Arts, 2003
Educational Outreach Director, Puppet Showplace Theater, 2001-2002
Teaching Artist, Cambridge Performance Project, 2002
Teaching Artist & Performer, Write to Change, 1996-1997, 2001
Puppeteer & Storyteller, We Three Puppetellers, 1999-2000
Workshop Presenter, International School of Tanganyika, 1999
After School Care Teacher, Cambridge Montessori School, 1998-1999
Curriculum Writer, Peace Games, 1999
Family Program Coordinator, Americorps, Peace Games, 1997-1998

Dr. Roald Hoffman

Dr. Roald Hoffman, a Nobel Prize–winning chemist, has a full writing life outside of his work in the sciences. His Web site— www.roaldhoffmann.com—opens with the line "Welcome to Roald Hoffmann's land between chemistry, poetry and philosophy," a fitting introduction to his many passions. Under the "biography" link, visitors can choose between a "short," "medium," or "long" bio. The short bio is reproduced here. If you want more details about his scientific life, or about his plays, poetry, and other writings, there are links for each of those too. Though a bio can cite Hoffmann's accomplishments and interests, a Web site is really the only way to present a more detailed look at his work.

Welcome to Roald Hoffmann's land between chemistry, poetry and philosophy.

LINKS:
Biography
Poetry
Science
Plays
Other Writing
Appearances
World of Chemistry
Entertaining Science
Interviews
Purchase Books
Download Articles
Forum
Contact

photo by Vivian Torrence

Biography:

Roald Hoffmann was born in 1937 in Zloczow, Poland. Having survived the war, he came to the U.S. in 1949, and studied chemistry at Columbia and Harvard Universities (Ph.D. 1962). Since 1965 he is at Cornell University, now as the Frank H. T. Rhodes Professor of Humane Letters. He has received many of the honors of his profession, including the 1981 Nobel Prize in Chemistry (shared with Kenichi Fukui).

"Applied theoretical chemistry" is the way Roald Hoffmann likes to characterize the particular blend of computations stimulated by experiment and the construction of generalized models, of frameworks for understanding, that is his contribution to chemistry.

Dr. Hoffmann is also a writer of essays, non-fiction, poems and plays. Two of his poetry collections, The *Metamict State* (1987) and *Gaps and Verges* (1990), have been published by the University Presses of Florida; *Memory Effects* was published in 1999 by the Calhoun Press of Columbia College, Chicago. At the end of 2002 two poetry collections were published by Roald Hoffmann: *Soliton*, by Truman State University Press, and a volume of selected poems translated into Spanish, *Catalista*.

In 1993 the Smithsonian Institution Press published *Chemistry Imagined*. A unique art/science/literature collaboration of Roald Hoffmann with artist Vivian Torrence, *Chemistry Imagined* reveals the creative and humanistic sparks of the molecular science. Spanish and Korean translations will appear soon. In 1995, Columbia University Press published *The Same and Not the Same*, a thoughtful account of the dualities that lie under the surface of chemistry. There are German, Spanish, Korean, Chinese, and Russian editions of this book, which has won a number of awards. In 1997 W.H. Freeman published *Old Wine, New Flasks: Reflections on Science and Jewish Tradition*, by Roald Hoffmann and Shira Leibowitz Schmidt, a book of the intertwined voices of science and religion. This book will be translated into Italian and Spanish. Dr. Hoffmann is also the presenter of a television course, *The World of Chemistry*, aired on many PBS stations and abroad.

The play *Oxygen*, by Carl Djerassi and Roald Hoffmann, premiered in the U.S. at the San Diego Repertory Theatre in 2001 and has had productions in London, East Lansing, MI, Madison, WI, Columbus, OH, Germany, Korea, Japan, New Zealand, and Toronto. *Oxygen* has been translated into many languages; it will be published in 2004 in Brazil in Portuguese by Lent and Vieira.

Michael Franco and Diane Curry

When innkeepers Michael Franco and Diane Curry, a married couple, decided to apply for a job as resident managers of a property in the Caribbean, they created a joint resume to show off their talents as a team. Since they both have other lives in the advertising field, they used their creative skills to come up with a unique document to showcase their shared experience as well as their personalities.

Diane Curry/Michael Franco

Churchtown Inn Experience

Conduct day-to-day guest relations including check-in/check-out, Inn tours, phone and email reservations and formal 4-course breakfast service for 9-room bed and breakfast with 2004 gross revenue exceeding $200,000. Perform concierge functions including orientation and map assistance; restaurant, attraction, movie and theater reservations; carriage ride bookings, and cultural information briefings.

Execute home improvement projects and repairs. Maintain garden, grounds and external aspects of Inn. Oversee grounds-maintenance staff and contractors. Develop staff training materials. Conceive of and coordinate multiple interior design and inn-improvement projects including installation of high-speed wireless Internet, painting of mural, bathroom remodeling, bedroom redesign, landscaping and more.

Successfully identified unsatisfied segment of tourist population in Lancaster County and expanded business by launching Amish Country Cottages: high-end, historic accommodations catering to sophisticated travelers as well as persons traveling with children or dogs.

Write and execute bulk list mailings including post-cards, newsletters, and email bulletins to announce Inn improvements, awards and events.

Develop and run special events such as Amish folklore weekends, murder mystery parties, German festivals, games weekends, scavenger hunts, holiday parties, Amish dinners and more.

Manage multiple aspects of our two additional vacation rental properties including accounts receivable, reservations, leases, website design and maintenance, advertising, utility management and more.

Maintain inventory for and run on-premises gift shop featuring sales of branded items, local-made crafts, books and other goods.

Michael's Additional Duties

Accurately maintain detailed guest database using guest-tracking software. Create projected and actual occupancy reports and segment guest list for promotional purposes.

Responsible for all Internet advertising including active weekly maintenance of online pay-per-click services. Improved ranking in major search engines and online directories such as TripAdvisor.com and dramatically increased inbound links. Wrote, designed and actively maintain Inn's website. Responsible for all photography featured on multiple web pages.

Manage accounts receivable/payable in excess of $200,000 per year. Balance monthly banking statements, pay monthly room and sales taxes as well as estimated quarterly payments to state and federal governments.

Diane's Additional Duties

Responsible for all aspects of housekeeping, menu planning and food preparation.

Maintain all guest rooms and common areas to a very high level of cleanliness and general repair. Purchase and maintain all linens and laundry equipment, maintain inventory of cleaning and household supplies and room amenities, schedule employees for seasonal fluctuations and special events.

Shop for and store all groceries, taking advantage of bulk efficiencies and local economies. Plan daily 4-course breakfasts in which no menu items are repeated for guests staying multiple days. Cater to special dietary needs and food allergies of guests. With simple applied creativity, managed to significantly improve food quality/variety and reduce expenses.

Contact, negotiate, train and supervise all housekeeping staff. Most staff and many contractors are Amish or Mennonite so sensitivity to cultural issues and working within social and religious boundaries is critical.

Researched and obtained permit for installation of new on-site septic system. This included interaction with engineers, soil scientists, township zoning officials, state regulators and system installers over a three year period. Installation date is July 2005. Amen.

Other Skills

Demonstrated ability to talk to a guest and take a reservation while preventing the lemon ginger muffins from burning and still managing to meet the Fed Ex man at the front door before the second ring!

The composure to look completely at ease and smile when a guest shows up two hours early for a room that's experiencing a major plumbing problem. Conversational skills and in-depth knowledge of local activities are a must!

The ability to answer the phone and sound ready to sell the beauty of our area no matter where on the property we are or how indisposed we may be. This includes the acquired knowledge that if the phone is not ringing or reservations are slow it must mean it is time to use the toilet! That one simple action always makes the phone ring.

The amazing patience required when a guest decides to "double-check" our printed directions to an area attraction, question if we're sure we know that's where it's located and proceed to suggest a better way. Breathe, don't sigh, smile. Repeat as needed.

The skill of staying power and pride of ownership: we'll do any job that needs doing, at any time it needs doing, whether or not we agree it needs doing, whether or not it's ever been our job before or ever will be again, whether or not we want to do it (coin-toss allowed) provided our actions will increase guest satisfaction and improve the appearance or functionality of our property. Scout's honor.

Deborah Epstein Henry

Deborah Epstein Henry is a lawyer/consultant who focuses on work/ life issues. As a lawyer, which is how she began her career, she had a traditional resume documenting her education, positions, and experience. Once her speaking and consulting practice grew, however, she realized that people were only interested in seeing a bio. Note that Henry's bio mentions the fact that she is the mother of three young children. In light of her work, which focuses primarily on work/family issues affecting lawyers and law firms, her being a parent is as important as any of her other credentials.

Deborah Epstein Henry Bio

Deborah Epstein Henry is the Founder and President of Flex-Time Lawyers LLC, a networking and support organization with a mailing list of over 1,800 lawyers who work a flexible and/or reduced schedule or seek a resource on work/life and women's issues in New York and Philadelphia. The mission of Flex-Time Lawyers LLC is to empower lawyers seeking work/life balance by: 1. providing support and career guidance; 2. facilitating networking; and 3. sharing information to effect change.

Debbie has garnered press coverage for her work in the area of work/life balance in the law from *The New York Times*, National Public Radio's Morning Edition and Radio Times, *The National Law Journal*, *New York Law Journal*, *ABA Journal*, *Philadelphia Business Journal*, Newsday, *The Philadelphia Inquirer*, *The Legal Intelligencer*, *Working Mother*, *Los Angeles Daily Journal*, *The Philadelphia Lawyer*, *The Pennsylvania Lawyer*, *Pittsburgh Post-Gazette*, *The Bencher*, *The Scarsdale Inquirer*, *Workforce Management*, *The Southampton Press*, *The Woman Advocate*, *Big Apple Parent*, and *Philadelphia Bar Reporter*.

Debbie is a commercial litigator and Of Counsel to the Philadelphia-based law firm of Schnader Harrison Segal & Lewis LLP. Debbie also is a consultant. She focuses on the issues of work/life balance and attorney retention, with a particular emphasis on retaining and promoting women lawyers. Debbie has an expertise in making flexible and reduced schedules and work/life balance a win-win situation for lawyers as well as their employers and clients. Her consulting approach includes: 1. drafting and analyzing part-time policies and providing recommendations to decision makers; 2. conducting individual sessions with management, partners, associates, administrators and/or committees to assess gender, diversity and work/life problem areas and solutions; 3. creating and furthering diversity and women's initiatives; and, 4. facilitating and leading seminars that provide strategies for improving the retention, promotion and overall status and satisfaction of women at their places of employment.

Debbie has experience counseling law firms, corporations and thousands of individual lawyers; speaking nationally in public forums; and, running nearly 100 Flex-Time Lawyers LLC meetings on these issues. She was named a 2004 Pennsylvania Lawyer on the Fast Track by American Lawyer Media. Debbie served on the "Hidden Brain Drain" Task Force for the Center for Work-Life Policy, which focuses on the retention and promotion of women and minorities. She is a consultant to the New York State Bar Association Special Committee on Balanced Lives in the Law.

She received her B.A. in Psychology from Yale University and her J.D. *cum laude* from Brooklyn Law School. Following law school, she clerked for the Honorable Jacob Mishler in the United States District Court for the Eastern District of New York. Debbie is married and the mother of three boys, ages 10, 8 and 4. For more information, please visit www.flextime lawyers.com.

Ann Guttman

For nearly twenty years Ann Guttman has maintained two full-blown careers, as a Realtor and a professional musician. The two complement each other nicely and Guttman has always been open about the importance of each of her careers. So open, in fact, that the bio she uses for her real estate work begins with a reference to her life in music. Interestingly, her bio also mentions her husband, who has his own slash as a psychoanalyst/musician/musical director of a band. As a Realtor, Guttman has found that revealing these kinds of details makes her more interesting to clients.

Ann Guttman Bio

Ann Robinson Guttman began playing the French horn relatively late in life, while a theater major at Pennsylvania State University. After graduating from Penn State, Ann continued her musical studies at the Yale School of Music, earning her Master's Degree in 1978. The next year, Ann got her first job as a French horn player in New York City playing with the Bolshoi Ballet, and she soon became an active presence in the city's musical life, playing in Broadway shows and on stage in Lincoln Center, Radio City Music Hall, and Carnegie Hall. Ann has been a part of the New York City Opera Orchestra, the American Symphony Orchestra, and the Long Island Philharmonic, and she has performed with the New York Philharmonic. Though New York City has been her home for 26 years, music has taken Ann around the globe, from Europe to the Far East, and she's played with some of the finest musicians in the world, including Itzhak Perlman, Yo-Yo Ma, Kurt Masur, James Levine, Placido Domingo, Kathleen Battle, and Marilyn Horne.

In 1984, when Ann became the chairperson of the Sales and Sublets Committee of the co-op where she lived, the excitement of real estate captivated her. In January 1992, a growing real estate company then known as Hunt Kennedy welcomed Ann to its roster of agents. Adding real estate pursuits to a busy music schedule, Ann quickly became a top producer in Hunt Kennedy's Westside office. In the ensuing years, she gained great experience in both "up" and "down" markets, selling co-ops and condominiums in every price range in every neighborhood of Manhattan. In September 2005, Ann was named Vice President and manager of the downtown office of Coldwell Banker Hunt Kennedy.

Ann resides on the Upper West Side with her husband, Steve, and their two dogs, Bam and Annabella. Steve is a musician who plays jazz trumpet and has been Musical Director of Blood, Sweat & Tears for the last 20 years. He is also a licensed psychoanalyst. Steve and Ann were married atop the Empire State Building on New Year's Day, 1992.

Dr. Robert Alper

Dr. Robert Alper is a rabbi/stand-up comic whose whole persona as a comic is informed by his identity as a rabbi. In the bio that appears on his Web site—www.bobalper.com—he addresses his slash in the first paragraph with a joke, referring to himself as "the world's only practicing clergyman doing stand-up comedy . . . intentionally."

BOB ALPER

WHO AM I?

Who Am I?

Books & CDs

Types of Shows

Performance Schedule

Reviews

Press Clippings

For Media Visitors

Bob Alper is the only rabbi in the country who regularly addresses congregations that require a cover charge and a two-drink minimum. Sound funny? You bet it is. Because Bob is **the world's only practicing clergyman doing stand-up comedy . . . intentionally.** His fresh, contemporary, and totally "unorthodox" style has been delighting audiences from Hollywood's **IMPROV** to **The Montreal Comedy Festival**. And his unique brand of intelligent, 100% clean humor appeals to everyone—from a synagogue or church crowd to corporate events, colleges, and theatres throughout North America and London.

"DON'T WORRY, RABBI, YOU'LL BE GREAT... AFTER ALL, YOU'VE HAD TWENTY YEARS EXPERIENCE IN FRONT OF A HOSTILE AUDIENCE."

A native of Providence, Rhode Island, Bob is a graduate of Lehigh University, was ordained at Hebrew Union College in Cincinnati, and is the first Jewish person ever to earn a doctorate from the Princeton Theological Seminary. He has served congregations in Buffalo and Philadelphia, where he continues to conduct High Holiday services.

Bob began his comedy career in 1986 when he entered the "Jewish Comic of the Year Contest" at the Going Bananas club in Philadelphia. Television, radio, and personal appearances followed as he quickly honed his distinctive approach to stand-up. He's been seen on *Good Morning America*, **Showtime**, the **BBC, CNN**, and was featured on *Extra*, TV's top-rated entertainment program, immediately following a segment on the size of Jennifer Lopez's buttocks.

Today, Bob performs nearly 100 shows per year, drawing tremendous audience numbers and response. His humor is fast-paced and sophisticated, yet gentle and unhurtful: all in all, a charming and affable comedian. In addition to his solo shows, Bob performs frequently in an extraordinary pairing with Muslim/Arab comedian Ahmed Ahmed.

Bob is the author of two books that further showcase his considerable talents: *Life Doesn't Get Any Better Than This*, an inspirational collection now in its fifth printing, and the award-winning full-color cartoon book *A Rabbi Confesses*. He's also produced two best-selling comedy CDs.

Bob resides in rural Vermont with his wife Sherri, a psychotherapist. They are empty-nest parents of Zack and Jessie.

1-888-483-3297
Info@BobAlper.com

Geoff

Geoff is a lawyer/actor-director who uses completely different resumes to showcase his different talents. If you were to look at his "actor" or "director" resume, you would almost have no idea that he's the same person profiled in his "lawyer" resume.

Geoff

(XXX) XXX.XXXX

<u>Hair/Eyes</u>:	Brown
<u>Height</u>:	5'9"
<u>Weight</u>:	150 lbs.

STAGE

LYSISTRATA 100	Cinesias's Servant	Untitled Theater #61, D ir. Edward Einhorn
GRIMM'S FAIRY TALES	King, Judge, Narrator	Atlantic Theater Co., Dir. Bridgette Dunlap
MEASURE FOR MEASURE	Friar Peter, Froth	Compass Rose Theater Co., Dir. John Castro
DEN OF THIEVES	Red	Word of Mouth, Dir. Seth Green
FIVE (The 24 Hour Plays)	Geoff	24 Hour Company, Dir. Kirk Jackson
YOU CAN COUNT ON ME	Terry	Atlantic Showcase, Dir. Anya Saffir
FRAME 312	*Assistant Director*	Atlantic Theater Co., Dir. Karen Kohlhaas
MAD FOREST	*Sound Design*	A.T.C.A.S., Dir. Anya Saffir
THE WINTER'S TALE	*Sound Design*	A.T.C.A.S., Dir. Anya Saffir

FILM

ANNA ON THE NECK	Mr. Barker	Ind., Dir. Gary Schwartz
BETTER THINGS	Green Hat Man	Colum. Un., Dir. Ryan Gomez
MARGARITA HAPPY HOUR	Ed	Ind./Sundance Film Festival, Dir. Ilya Chiaken

TELEVISION

MIRACLE'S BOYS	Hooded Messenger	MTv, Dir. Lavar Burton
THE GRAHAM NORTON EFFECT	Hair Game	Chealsea Studios
THE GANG	Worm	UCLA Film/TV, Dir. Larry Silverberg

TRAINING

ATLANTIC THEATER COMPANY ACTING SCHOOL
  -Professional Program
  -Summer Intensive (with Scott Zigler of A.R.T.)

SITI COMPANY
  -Spring Training
  -Saratoga Summer Intensive (with Anne Bogart)
  -Advanced Training

UPRIGHT CITIZENS BRIGADE
  -Improvisation, long form

SPECIAL SKILLS

Fight Choreography; Spanish (conversational); Scuba Diving (PADI certified); Emergency Medical Technician (NY); Yoga; Can carry a tune

GEOFF
[address redacted]

<u>Phone</u>:   <u>E-Mail</u>:

WORK EXPERIENCE

THEATER

Production Director: 2005-present
Atlantic Theater Company Acting School

Recent work includes:

<u>DIRECTOR</u>: *Love and How to Cure It* by Thornton Wilder (director); *Stars* by Romulus Linney (director); *Frame 312* by Keith Reddin (assistant director to Karen Kohlhaas*)*; *Blue/Orange* (production assistant)

<u>LITERARY</u>: Assisting Literary Mangers at both the Atlantic Theater Company and New York Theater Workshop.

<u>SOUND DESIGN</u>*: Street Scene* by Elmer Rice; *Mad Forest* by Caryl Churchill*; The Winter's Tale*; *No Exit* by Jean-Paul Sartre; *Bobby Gould in Hell* by David Mamet

<u>ACTOR</u>: *Stage: Lysistrata* (untitled theater company)*; Grimm's Fairy Tales* (ATC)*; Measure for Measure* (Compass Rose)*; Den of Thieves* (Word of Mouth)*; Five* (The 24 Hour Plays); *You Can Count on Me* (Atlantic Showcase); *Film: Anna on the Neck* (forthcoming independent); *Better Things* (Columbia University); *Margarita Happy Hour* (Sundance Film Festival); *The Gang* (UCLA Film/TV)

FREELANCE WRITER

Recently published work includes:

"Off the Streets," *The New York Times*, May 2, 2001; "Second Thoughts," *The New York Times,* March 7, 2001; "Second Wind," *The New York Times*, November 15, 2000; "Time to Hunker Down," *The New York Times*, September 6, 2000; "Confessions Of A Temp," *The American Lawyer*, October 1999; "The Footnote, " *New Orleans Review*, Vol. 23, No. 1; <u>A New Deal for Free Speech: Free Speech and the Labor Movement in the 1930s</u>, *Virginia Law Review*, Vol. 80, No. 1

THEATER TRAINING

Atlantic Theater Company Acting School
* Professional Program
* Vermont Summer Workshop with Scott Zigler

SITI Company
* Summer Intensive with Anne Bogart
* Multiple Advanced Suzuki/Viewpoints Workshops with SITI Company

Upright Citizens Brigade
* Long-form Improvisation Levels I-III

EDUCATION

University of Virginia Law School (Charlottesville, VA) JD with honors

University of Virginia Graduate School (Charlottesville, VA) MA, History

University of California at Los Angeles (LA, CA) BA Summa Cum Laude

Escuela Cabaguil, School of Spanish Language (Antigua, Guatemala) Certified

GEOFF
[Address redacted]

Phone: FAX: E-Mail:

WORK EXPERIENCE

ATTORNEY   **Weil, Gotshal & Manges** (New York, NY)   1996–2001

- Education policy and litigation, trademark law, entertainment law, international arbitration;

- Pro Bono advocacy on behalf of New York public schools;

- Pro Bono advocacy on behlaf of families of victims of 9/11;

- Extensive legal research and writing, oral advocacy, settlement negotiation, depositions and advising of clients.

Davis, Graham & Stubbs (Denver, CO)   1994–1995

- Legal research and writing; taking of depositions; advising clients

FREELANCE   *Recently published work includes:*
WRITER

- "Off the Streets," *The New York Times*, May 2, 2001.

- "Second Thoughts," *The New York Times,* March 7, 2001.

- "Second Wind," *The New York Times*, November 15, 2000.

- "Time to Hunker Down," *The New York Times*, September 6, 2000.

- "Confessions Of A Temp," *The American Lawyer*, October 1999

- "The Footnote, " *New Orleans Review*, Vol. 23, No. 1

- A New Deal for Free Speech: Free Speech and the Labor Movement in the 1930s, *Virginia Law Review*, Vol. 80, No. 1

VOLUNTEER
TEACHER   **Institute for Collaborative Education**   2000–present

- Teaching classes exploring issues of criminal and constitutional law with high school students

- Curriculum design and modification.

EDUCATION

University of Virginia Law School (Charlottesville, VA)   JD
– *Awards/Activities*:
- *Virginia Law Review*
  ▸Editorial Board (1992-93)
  ▸Articles Review Board (1993-94)
- Student/Faculty Round Table
- Order of the Coif (top 5%)

University of Virginia Graduate School (Charlottesville, VA)   MA, History
- Thesis: A New Deal for Free Speech: Free Speech and the Labor Movement in the 1930s, Published: *Virginia Law Review*, Vol. 80-1.

University of California at Los Angeles (Los Angeles, CA)   BA
– *Awards/Activities*:
- Summa Cum Laude
- National Debate Champions 1990; Runners-up 1989 & 1991
- Co-Captain of the UCLA Speech and Debate Team

Escuela Cabaguil, School of Spanish Language (Antigua, Guatemala)   Certified, 1995

MEMBERSHIPS   Colorado Bar; New York Bar; American Bar Association; ABCNY.

INTERESTS   Talking, writing, acting, travel.

References and/or letters of recommendation available upon request

NOTES / / / / /

Chapter 1: The Slash Mind-set
1. Herminia Ibarra, *Working Identities* (Boston: Harvard Business School Press, 2003), p. 10, Preface.

Chapter 2: Slash Breeding Grounds
1. Rabbi Maurice Lamm, "Is Life After 55 Going to Be Just Another Pumpernickel?" *The Los Angeles Times* (April 15, 1985).
2. Thomas Vinciguerra, "Stars of Stage, Screen . . . and Freshman Biology," *The New York Times* (September 11, 2005).

Chapter 3: Thinking Like a Modern Moonlighter
1. *Beyond the Basics: Techniques for the Serious Seller*, eBay University (eBay Inc., 2005), pp. 1-5.
2. Anna Bahney, "Hi, My Name Is Sam, and I'll Be Your Broker," *The New York Times* (September 5, 2004).

Chapter 7: Synergies, Leveraging, and the Power of Incongruous Combinations
1. Tim Green, *The Dark Side of the Game* (New York: Warner Books, 1996): p. 129.

Chapter 8: Working the Twenty-first Century Workplace
1. See www.resourcesglobalprofessional.com (accessed March 27, 2006).
2. Erin White and Jeffrey A. Trachtenberg, "Sabbaticals: The Pause That Refreshes," *The Wall Street Journal* (August 2, 2005); Alan R. Earls, "Sabbaticals Aren't Just for Academia Anymore," *The Boston Globe* (May 8, 2005).
3. See "About Us" on www.ignitionventures.com (accessed March 27, 2006).
4. Sylvia Ann Hewlett, Carolyn Buck Luce, and Cornel West, "Leadership in Your Midst," *Harvard Business Review* (November 2005).
5. Jody Miller and Matt Miller, "Get a Life," *Fortune* (November 28, 2005).

Chapter 9: Overcoming Overload, Naysayers, and Other Slash Stumbling Blocks
1. Tim Green, *The Dark Side of the Game* (New York: Warner Books, 1996): pp. 123–124.
2. Katharine Q. Seelye and Scotte Shane, "A Star with Multiple Roles Now Faces Questions of Conflict Among Them," *The New York Times* (November 17, 2005).
3. Susan Saulny, "Truant Teacher Who Lost Job Finds His Revenge in the Ring," *The New York Times* (August 12, 2005).

Chapter 10: Special Considerations for Parent Slashes
1. Michelle Conlin, "The Rise of the Mompreneurs," *BusinessWeek* (June 7, 2004).

INDEX /////

ABOUT THE AUTHOR //////

Marci Alboher, a former lawyer, is a writer/speaker/coach living in New York City. Marci's writing focuses primarily on workplace and career issues. She is a regular contributor to the *New York Times*, and her work has also appeared in publications such as *Time Out New York*, *Travel and Leisure*, the *Chronicle of Philanthropy*, and *Legal Affairs*. Marci is a member of the faculty of the New York Writers Workshop, where she teaches journalism. She frequently speaks at national conferences and career-related events, and privately coaches writing clients and professionals in transition. For more information, visit www.heymarci.com.

Nov. 24
Shirley Chisolm
Day
White House Project